Tao in Ten

Ten Easy
Lessons Series

Tao in Ten

C. Alexander Simpkins, Ph.D.

&

Annellen M. Simpkins, Ph.D.

Tuttle Publishing
Boston · Rutland, VT · Tokyo

First published in 2002 by Tuttle Publishing, an imprint of Periplus Editions (HK) Ltd., with editorial offices at 153 Milk Street, Boston, Massachusetts 02109.

Library of Congress Cataloging-in-Publication Data

Simpkins, C. Alexander.
    Tao in ten / C. Alexander Simpkins & Annellen M. Simpkins
        p. cm. — (Ten easy lessons series)
    Includes bibliographic references.
    ISBN: 0–8048–3451–2 (pbk.)
        1. Taoism. 2. Hygiene, Taoist. I. Simpkins, Annellen M. II. Title. III. Series.

BL1920 . S548 2002
299'.51444—dc21   2002023687

Distributed by:

North America
Tuttle Publishing
Distribution Center
Airport Industrial Park
364 North Clarendon, VT 05759-9436
Tel: (802) 773-8930
Fax: (802) 773-6993
Email: info@tuttlepublishing.com

Asia Pacific
Berkeley Books Pte. Ltd.
130 Joo Seng Road
#06-01/03 Olivine Building
Singapore 368357
Tel: (65) 6280-1330
Fax: (65) 6280-6290
Email: inquiries@periplus.com.sg

Japan
Tuttle Publishing
Yaikari Building, 3rd Floor
5-4-12 Ōsaki
Shinagawa-ku, Tokyo
Japan 141 0032
Tel: (03) 5437-0171
Fax: (03) 5437-0755
Email: tuttle-sales@gol.com

First edition
07 06 05 04 03   9 8 7 6 5 4 3 2

Design by Dutton & Sherman Design
Printed in Canada

We dedicate this book to:

*Our parents, Carmen and Nathaniel Simpkins and
Naomi and Herbert Minkin,*

Our children, Alura Aguilera and C. Alexander Simpkins Jr.,

*And to the Taoist sages through the ages whose wisdom
points us to the Tao.*

Contents

Preface

As society becomes more complex and sophisticated, people find that they lose touch with their simpler, deeper nature. The ancient philosophy of Taoism, however, can point you back to what is truly important. Taoism can guide you in finding your Way; it can help you develop yourself fully and become the best person you can be. New and creative options open up when you are One with Tao.

About This Book

Tao in Ten offers a way to experience Taoism and apply it to your life. Ultimately, Taoism is experienced on a personal level, and this is when the greatest benefits are found.

This book presents fundamental teachings from Taoism in ten easy lessons. Each lesson gives experiences and understandings of a key Taoist principle, revealing the infinite potentials for better living at One with Tao.

Themes, however, are reflected in more than one lesson because Taoism does not represent ideas as separate, distinct categories. It is a holistic theory, one in which you will recognize counterparts and parallels between themes. Be open and flexible in your thinking and let your associations flow, as these are your inroads into Tao.

How to Use This Book

Read each section and then try the exercises. We encourage you to think about each idea, consider how it relates to your life, and experiment with the understandings. As you learn more about Taoism, new possibilities emerge, opening up richer and fuller ways for living.

Begin with what comes naturally. This applies to all the exercises in the book, many of which include meditation. There is no right or wrong place for meditation. Where you meditate should feel right to you. People usually prefer a quiet place where they will not be disturbed for a time. With practice, however, you will be able to meditate almost anywhere. Remember to sit comfortably. Traditionally, people sit on a cushion on the floor when they meditate, and this can be a very effective position. But if you are not comfortable on the floor, a chair will do just as well.

Begin meditating for one or two minutes. You can set the timer on your watch or simply stop when you feel ready. Novices sometimes believe that they must meditate for a long time. But you can also find your way into meditation gradually, beginning with only a few minutes a day. What is important is that you meditate regularly. Practice helps, as it does in many things.

As you embark on the Path, new potentials will open up. Be patient and enjoy the journey!

Introduction

Historical Background
of Taosim

Tao is all pervading
And its use is inexhaustible.
　　　　—*Tao Te Ching*, Chapter Four

Lao-tzu

Lao-tzu (b. 604 B.C.) is the legendary founder of Taoism and is said to
have been born in Cheu, which translates as the State of Everywhere.
Master Chinese historian Ssu-ma Ch'ien (145–86 B.C.) indicated that
Lao-tzu's actual identity and personal history is mysterious, like the
Tao itself. According to legend, Lao-tzu was born old, having been
carried for sixty years in his mother's womb. He lived on Bramble Lane
and is believed to have been the archivist of the Royal Library.
Confucius, who was fifty years younger than Lao-tzu, consulted Lao-
tzu and considered him a consummate source of wisdom. After many
years in the city, Lao-tzu became discouraged with all the corruption
he saw about him. He decided to seek peace and tranquillity in the
country. Before walking through the northwest gate, Lao-tzu told the

gatekeeper his poetic principles, which he called the *Tao Te Ching*, and, fortunately for posterity, the gatekeeper wrote them down. The gatekeeper was so taken with what he heard that he decided to join Lao-tzu in his journey, leaving the writings behind. Lao-tzu disappeared, never to be found. Some say he converted the Buddha, others that he became Buddha. Taoism's belief in the potential for immortality, engendered by Lao-tzu's disappearance, continues to this day.

The *Tao Te Ching* is a short work, only five thousand words, yet it has had a profound impact on people through the ages. Hundreds of translations and interpretations of the *Tao Te Ching* continue to be made. In 1973, another version was found in a cave in Ma-wang-tui, Central China, that dates back to 168 B.C. It is the oldest known edition. The order of chapters in the Ma-wang-tui text is different from traditional interpretations—the Tao chapters follow the Te chapters. But such ambiguity and mystery is completely in character with the *Tao Te Ching*. In the lessons here, however, we have followed the traditional order, which begins with Tao.

Chuang-tzu

Chuang-tzu (369–286 B.C.) was the second major figure in Taoist philosophical history. He wrote or inspired the writing of two long volumes of stories illustrating and teaching in accord with Lao-tzu. Known as the *Chuang-tzu*, these stories emphasize Taoist values and lifestyle choices in accordance with Tao. Chuang-tzu is considered a kind of patron saint to artists and craftsmen since he believed in and often used artists and craftsmen as examples of Taoist principles. He is also highly regarded and quoted by Zen Buddhists since his values were similar to theirs.

Chuang-tzu was from the family of Chou and was a native of the Meng district. He was a satirist and storyteller rather than a poetic mystic, and so he often contrasted Lao-tzu's concepts with those of Confucianism, a rival philosophy. Chuang-tzu wrote imaginatively of Confucius and Lao-tzu engaged in dialogue—Lao-tzu always appearing as the wiser one.

Lieh-tzu

Lieh-tzu (fourth century B.C.) was another important founding figure in early classical Taoism. His writings, known as *The Book of Lieh-tzu*, include stories and theoretical sections that expanded Taoism further, even into dreams and altered states, showing that Taoism is a viable, broad system of thought. His stories are insightful and filled with advice. He was respectful to other philosophies as well.

Originally named Lieh Yu-k'on, Lieh-tzu spent his early life in Cheng; eventually, he moved to the state of Wei. His ideas and writings were probably compiled by his followers at a later time, as was the custom. Thus, passages are sometimes shared with Chuang-tzu, who refers to him in his writings. Lieh-tzu's writings were interpreted with commentaries by Chang Chan, an officer during the Chin dynasty (221–207 B.C.). These commentaries helped make sense of Lieh-tzu's thoughts. Modern scholars often include them as part of their understandings.

Neo-Taoists

Taoism continued to blend with many aspects of Chinese philosophy and cultural life. The Neo-Taoists (A.D. 220–420) were a group of intellectual freethinkers who lived during a time when Confucianism was dominant and Buddhism was growing. They reinterpreted the dialogues between Lao-tzu and Confucius to mean that Confucianism and Taoism were compatible. In fact, since Confucius studied with Lao-tzu, his principles could be understood through Taoism. The Neo-Taoists believed that Confucius did not mention Tao because he revered it in the proper spirit of silence. The Neo-Taoists blended aspects of the *I Ching*, *The Book of Changes*, Buddhism, and Confucianism together with Taoism.

The Pure Conversation School was the most well known of the Neo-Taoist groups. Some of its prominent members were Liu Yang (221–300), Wang Hui-chih (d. 338), and Wang Pi (226–249), who died at the age of twenty-four after an intense life of Tao. These Neo-

Taoists were known as free spirits for living spontaneously with open minds. They spent a great deal of time out in nature. Some did translations, such as Wang Pi, whose commentary on the *Tao Te Ching* is still being read and used today for its wise perspective and depth.

Taoist Alchemy

Alchemy emerged gradually in China to seamlessly join with Taoism. Tsou Yen (305–240 B.C.) expressed a theory, known as the Five Elements, that was one of the bases for alchemy. He thought that earth, wind, metal, fire, and water were the five fundamental elements in the universe. Each element restrains or overcomes another element while each element also promotes or stimulates another element. Thus, the interaction among elements is continual transformation and change.

Tsou Yen gave us an illustration, known as the Five Elements Diagram, to show the dynamic interrelationships among the elements. Used in Taoism, this diagram was employed widely in medicine, martial arts, the arts, Feng Shui, and even politics (see the Five Elements Diagram in Lesson Four).

Tsou Yen's theory naturally led to practical alchemical applications for transforming one thing into another. His followers experimented with compounds and elements, such as cinnabar, which was believed to be an important ingredient to transform mortal human beings into immortal beings. The Taoist alchemists tried to create an elixir of immortality.

These practitioners of Taoist alchemy were known as Fang Shih, formula masters. Some used rituals, rites, charts, and magic along with the alchemical elixirs in their efforts to bring about changes. The Fang Shih were similar to tantric practitioners in Tibetan Buddhism and Japanese Shingon. Though they came from different philosophical bases, they all incorporated a system of symbols and formulas as a shortcut to the benefits of enlightenment, such as long life, good health, amazing memory, happiness, and personal powers.

One famous Neo-Taoist philosopher and alchemist was Ko Hung (A.D. 283–343), who wrote a pharmacopoeia in A.D. 317 called the *P'ao P'u Tsu* of alchemy, detailing ingredients, compounds, and techniques for their correct use.

Many of the metals and compounds used in the elixirs were poisons—for example, cinnabar contains mercury—and a number of the early alchemists died. Eventually, because of its dangers, Taoist alchemy with real materials fell into disuse. However, some useful substances were studied and catalogued, such as gunpowder for firearms and cinnabar for red paint pigment. The science of chemistry evolved from these roots.

A new trend called symbolic alchemy gradually took hold in the third century as a substitute for physical alchemy, a shift that has contributed to many Taoist practices still in use today. Symbols were substituted for the dangerous, toxic substances, keeping the formulae and methods as a metaphor for transformation. Thus the cauldron that heated the potions referred to the inner fire within, located in certain energy centers of the body. Breathing techniques were developed to raise body heat (chi energy). Different elements contained in the elixirs became meditation methods for self-transformation, such as visualization and the slow movements of chi kung and tai chi.

Religious Taoism

Taoism also developed into a religion that traced its inspiration back to Lao-tzu and the *Tao Te Ching*. Religious themes were implied in the early philosophical Taoist writings but were made explicit around the first century A.D. Lao-tzu was elevated in spiritual status, from a mortal man into a deity, merging him with earlier mythologies and the occult sciences of the Yellow Emperor, considered the first doctor as well as a great leader. Eastern medicine grew out of this merging of Taoist philosophy with medical practices developed by the religious Taoists.

A Taoist church was formed and small sects began to grow, promising people a better life through healthy, moral living. These groups became powerful and influential, eventually gathering armies and many followers. By A.D. 184, most of China practiced the Taoist religion. They established a lineage of Taoist popes, passed down along family lines. The Taoist religion continues to this day, with followers in many places around the world.

There are many streams of Taoism that flowed as tributaries into the sea of Tao, but for our purposes, Taoism is one great ocean, unified in the Tao.

Begin with Tao

When the Tao is followed,
Power and virtue become one.
Find the way that is elusive and unknowable,
Effortless and everywhere.
                    —*Tao Te Ching* 21, Grigg 1995, 86

Before You Begin

For thousands of years people have found inspiration and strategies for living healthy and fulfilling lives by being in tune with Tao. Taoism offers a unique perspective, a frame of reference within which to live. This point of view is different from how we usually look at things. Those new to Taoism might have difficulty understanding Taoist concepts and ways of thinking because these ideas are different from the Western frame of reference. But you can add the Taoist perspective and all the new possibilities it brings as a supplement to your life.

This analogy may help: Maps offer a way to understand how to find your way around a strange territory. For example, an elevation map will show you how the terrain looks, where the mountains and valleys are located. If you plan to go mountain climbing, an elevation map will guide your path. However, if you want the shortest route to a destination, an elevation map will be of no use. A road map will be far more helpful.

Taoism uses different maps than are used in the West to describe and depict certain aspects of our universe, including the earth and human beings. Both Eastern and Western maps depict things that are really there, but they point to different phenomena. For example, Eastern medicine maps show patterns of energy systems, whereas Western medicine maps show organ systems.

We encourage you to explore a different map of your territory—your world of experience and how you understand yourself and your environment. When combined with the maps you already use, you will find that Taoism opens the doors of perception onto new vistas of possibilities.

Change

Taoism holds that everything is always changing. The world we know, that we grew up expecting always to be the same, changes. Boundaries between countries are shifting; even the names of countries can be different from one year to another. Consult an atlas of this year and compare the names and boundaries in Europe and Africa to an atlas from thirty years ago and you will see many changes.

What we learn and study is also changing. Courses in computer science as a separate discipline were not even offered fifteen years ago. Concepts of matter and energy that were hypothetical in the twentieth century are being accepted in the twenty-first. For example, a new state of matter called the Bose-Einstein condensate (BEC), was hypothesized by Einstein in the 1920s, but was only recently created experimentally. In this state, it becomes impossible to distinguish between separate atoms: all is truly one.

The homes we live in have new standards and codes of construction. Newer appliances no longer look or act in quite the same way they did in previous decades. Often they do a better job while also conserving energy and other resources.

Contemporary music, reflecting the times, is vastly different, though there may be nostalgia for the past. Our vocabulary, patterns of spoken language, even the tones and expressions we use have all changed. Society has changed, incorporating different standards and expectancies. And we have changed. When we look in a mirror we can't help but see the changes. Everything that exists eventually passes into nonexistence.

Western tradition has some parallels to this Taoist idea of change. The great Greek philosopher Heraclites around 500 B.C. said, "You never step into the same river twice." The parallels between Eastern and Western thought are clearly seen with Heraclites' idea that life is movement and that it develops through the conflict of opposites. Out of this conflicting chaos emerges a harmony, the Logos.

I Ching, The Book of Changes

The Chinese recognized thousands of years ago that life is continually undergoing transformation. They expressed this view in a book called I Ching, The Book of Changes. The I Ching has become a classic reference for Taoism and for Confucianism, explaining the transitory nature of our existence. The book's various sections are a collection of many authors, spanning centuries of time. Scholars believe the book may have been compiled by King Wen, the founder of the Chou dynasty (1150–249 B.C.). The additional texts, known as "Wings," are ascribed to Confucius. Although scholars are not certain that Confucius was the author, these chapters are clearly Confucian in their philosophical orientation. What we can be certain of is that thousands of years went into the writing and organizing of the I Ching, helping to give it the rich multileveled significance that can be found in its pages today.

The I Ching, The Book of Changes includes many Taoist ideas. Primarily among them is the idea of simplicity. "The good that lies in the easy and the simple makes it correspond to the highest kind of existence" (*I Ching*, Wilhelm 1995, 24). The book points out that when we observe the simple qualities of our experience we cannot help but notice that everything is changing. Only by conceptualizing—stepping away from the simple—do we begin to fabricate a solid world of enduring reality. The *I Ching*, like Taoism, encourages us to turn back to our natural, simple perception so that we can see what is really there: constant change.

The book distinguishes three kinds of changes. The first is cyclical transformation, where one thing changes into another thing but eventually is restored to its original form. An example of cyclical change is the seasons, in which summer inevitably becomes fall, then winter, spring, and back to summer again, repeating in a cycle over and over.

A second type of change is progressive development. Transformation takes place a little at a time. Each new form contains the previous, always moving forward. A life span is a good example of progressive development. We are born, we live, growing older and older, and then we die.

The immutable law that works through the other transformations is the third type of change. Change begins small, almost unnoticeable. But as things go through their transformations, changes multiply exponentially, with enormous results. For example, if you look at your neighborhood from one day to the next you might not notice much difference. But if you left for a number of years and then returned, you would see many changes. The *I Ching* points out that even heaven and earth began small and evolved over eons to become the complex universe we experience today. One of the famous diagrams that shows the transformations on a universal scale is the wu chi, tai chi diagram (see page 11).

The Tao

But still, deep within, there is an underlying stability, a unity, an essence that, though we cannot see it, we know is there. Though we change day by day, when we look in the mirror, we know the person

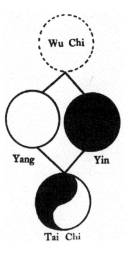

Wu Chi, Tai Chi

we see. Our friends, our family, go through many changes as they pass through life, yet we recognize an unchanging essence. There is a unity at the root and beyond all change. Taoism knows this as Tao.

> The Tao that can be told of
> Is not the Absolute Tao;
> The Names that can be given
> Are not Absolute Names
> —*Tao Te Ching* 1, Yutang 1942, 583

Tao is nameless. If you call it something, it hides. But people needed some way to refer to it, so they called it Tao. Language shows the intimately fundamental nature of Tao. In China, streets are called Tao, pointing to one of Taoism's central meanings: Tao gives us a path to follow, known as the Way.

Tao cannot be named or conceived of because it is before concepts, before individual things. Tao is the pattern within patterns, the form within forms. For example, numbers express a certain type of order. Relations of mathematics express the sum of the underlying relations in our universe. Whenever we use numbers and symbols to express these relations, we are approaching Tao. But Tao itself always transcends our efforts to pin it down. A number exists by virtue of the universe of numbers—because they are.

Tao is the innate, fundamental essence. Order is already there, it need not be imposed. By returning to the root we gain the essence is a teaching of the *Tao Te Ching*. So return to the source, the wellspring of all existing things, by releasing. Letting go leads to Tao. Seek the inner pattern.

The Qualities of Tao

> Water is like the highest good
> because it flows to the lowest places.
> While people strive to move upward,
> water goes freely downward,
> And on its effortless course
> nourishes everything in its path.
> Such is the way of the Tao.
> —*Tao Te Ching* 8, Grigg 1995, 69

Tao is like water, flexible, yielding, but relentless. Mysteriously its essence is fluid, like water. And like a stream of water, if an obstacle impedes Tao's progress, it goes around it. Whether we conceive of Tao in terms of events, people, nature, action, or nonaction, Tao continues to flow unceasingly, coursing like a river toward an unknown destiny.

Like water, Tao fills any vessel in which it is contained, taking on the shape of the vessel. Pour water into another vessel, it takes on the new shape. Its form is a reflection of the object, so, too, with Tao.

> The Tao is empty (like a bowl)
> It may be used but its capacity is never exhausted.
>
> —*Tao Te Ching* 4, Chan 1963, 141

Tao is empty, like space. Contain space and you have something useful. For example, bowls, cups, boxes, and houses are all useful spaces. But once we fill them, their usefulness is defined, limited, even used up. A cup is most useful when it is empty. This concept was the key to Frank Lloyd Wright's architecture: Start from within. Begin with space. Build around space, don't try to create space from without, by making buildings.

But Tao is more profound than this. Tao is before being or nonbeing; it is prior to them both. Tao is the way in, Tao is the way out. Tao is the Way, the Path, and the standard before standards. Tao is the source, the wellspring of Oneness. From Tao comes the One. The overall pattern of wholeness is a function of Tao. Sequence and association are expressions of Tao.

Form and Formlessness

> The term *Nonbeing* indicates the beginning of heaven and earth; the term *Being* indicates the mother of the ten thousand things.
>
> For indeed, it is through the constant alteration between Nonbeing and Being that the wonder of the one and the limitation of the other will be seen.
>
> These two, having a common origin, are names with different terms.
>
> What they have in common is called the Mystery, the Mystery of Mysteries, the Gate of all Wonders.
>
> —*Tao Te Ching* 1, Duyvendak 1992, 17

Computers have revolutionized the world. To George Boole, the creator of Boolean algebra, the mathematical logic of computers, symbols can be used to represent relationships between being and nonbeing:

One—unity or universe—and Nothing—eternity. In our relationship to these contrasting ultimates, we discover deeper truth: the laws of Mind. And the basic number is one. From Tao comes the One, from One comes the universe. Tao's unchanging, formless essence takes on forms as yin becomes yang. But Tao does not actively remain as form. Tao returns to its source just as water seeks its own level. Spill a cup of water and the water no longer keeps its cup shape—it takes on the shape of the ground, but rounded; Tao is circular, rounded, natural. The universe begins from nothing and ends as nothing, only to change again and be transformed into something else. Our Western tradition of physics conceives of this in terms of decay that is random but cease-less. All becomes nothing. We cannot know Tao, only its changing momentary expression.

Meditation Points the Way to Tao

The Tao offers a valuable resource for all aspects of living in its mys-terious essence. When we attune ourselves to Tao, all of the untapped potential of Tao becomes accessible. Then life flows as it should and everything works out without obstruction. But how can we attune our-selves to something as elusive and undefined as Tao? The answer is simple: meditation.

Meditation is an ancient practice, so highly valued around the world that it has been called an inward "art." The essence of medita-tion is an inner experience. Taoists believe that when you turn your attention to your deeper inner being you will discover Tao. Meditation can show you how.

Taoist meditation begins by letting go of the external influences and thoughts. Like peeling an apple, layer by layer can be removed until you are left with the core, containing the seeds for beginnings and new growth. This meditation series will point you toward Tao so that you can experiment with a new attunement on the Taoist Path.

Discovering Tao

Meditation is a natural experience that everyone has had spontaneously for fleeting moments in life, moments of calm, clear focus. You can bring about this natural capacity of meditation by removing what interferes with it.

Chuang-tzu expressed this concept in a story. One day a student knocked on Chuang-tzu's door. The student had heard of Chuang-tzu's great wisdom from other teachers and had traveled a great distance to learn. He had studied many forms of philosophy, always seeking to add to his understandings. Chuang-tzu answered the door and the student said, "I am an ardent student of philosophy and I have heard that you are very knowledgeable. Will you take me on as your student?"

Chuang-tzu answered, "Only if you tell all the people you brought with you to leave."

The student turned around to see who had followed him to Chuang-tzu's house but was surprised to see no one else around. At first the student was mystified, but then he understood what Chuang-tzu was telling him. Before he could learn, he had to let go of the outer concerns he carried in his mind to allow his inner nature to be nourished. We all carry with us the conditioning we received from our culture, including our attitudes and beliefs. Many of these ideas come from our upbringing, schooling, the groups we are in, and the country in which we live. Taoists encourage us to set external concerns aside to open the way for Tao.

Meditation One: Begin Where You Are

Sit quietly with your eyes closed and relax for a few minutes. Notice your surroundings: the sounds around you, the temperature of the air, the quality of the light. Next, turn your attention to your thoughts. Pay attention to what you are thinking without getting too involved in any particular thought. Notice if you are feeling anything—happy, sad, irritated, tense, calm. Then, without trying to alter anything, can you allow your concerns to drop away for a moment, leaving you calmly at rest, without thought or concern? Just let it all go. Experience a quiet moment.

Emptiness Meditations

The *Tao Te Ching* says: "Take emptiness to the limit; Maintain tranquillity in the center" (*Tao Te Ching* 16, Henricks 1989, 68).

When you make yourself empty, you are One with Tao. After you have been able to feel some calming, try this exercise.

Emptiness Meditation I

Sit quietly with your eyes closed for a few minutes. Imagine that you are watching a large body of water, either a lake or the ocean. As you look, can you see the rhythmical movement of the waves and the gentle rippling of the water? The view is very peaceful and you find yourself relaxing as you watch. Don't try to relax, but don't interfere with relaxation as it happens. Continue to watch the water until you feel distractions falling away of themselves. With practice you will experience emptiness—open, receptive readiness, calm and at ease.

Emptiness Meditation II

Sit quietly with your eyes closed. Notice your thoughts as they occur but do not take a stand about them. Simply notice each thought, then let it go. If you find yourself following a line of thought, let it go. Like sitting on the bank of a river and watching the leaves float past, you let the leaves go. Eventually the leaves of your thoughts will lessen, then stop, leaving you with emptiness, only the stream of your consciousness flowing ever onward to the sea.

Attuning to Your True Nature

Man models himself after Earth.
Earth models itself after Heaven.
Heaven models itself after Tao.
And Tao models itself after Nature.
—*Tao Te Ching* 25, Chan 1963, 152–153

Nature and the natural way are the wellsprings of Tao. By understanding the Ways of nature and our own human nature, you discover Tao. Nature can become a guiding beacon to Tao.

The Tao of Nature

Tao expresses itself in nature. Plants know how to grow and when to flower. Rosebushes produce roses and violet plants always yield violets. Animals live their lives expressing their natures and fulfilling their destiny. Birds fly and horses gallop. But birds are never plagued by doubts because they can't gallop, nor do horses feel inferior because they can't fly. If you have ever had a pet that had babies, you saw the

Tao in action: The mother gave birth and took care of her offspring without any assistance. All in nature know exactly what to do and they do it.

Taoists believe that human beings also possess the instincts for life and fulfillment. But people often interfere with the natural course of their lives. They alienate themselves from their true being, getting in the way of the natural flow. Learning to follow the Tao of nature can bring you back to the natural flow toward fulfillment.

Observing Nature

You can learn about Tao in nature by observing nature itself. Nature doesn't hide—it reveals its ways to us if we are willing to take the time to notice. Go out into nature, perhaps in a park, at the beach, or even in your own yard.

Pick something to watch—perhaps a plant or a small insect. Notice how the plant moves with the wind, how a flower opens toward the sun, how the insect moves along. Observe an animal at play, perhaps a pet.

If you can relate to the world better through sound (e.g., those who are always listening to music) you might prefer to listen to nature. Close your eyes and hear the birds sing, the wind blow, or whatever you sense.

Think about how everything in nature expresses itself just as it is.

Your environmental context is part of your identity. If you take a fish out of water to admire it, the fish dies. Fish live comfortably in their water environment, yet if you have ever started your own fish tank, you know that keeping fish alive in an artificial environment is challenging. Only when you are able to create the correct balance of bacteria and clean water with correct temperature and chemistry do the fish thrive.

Human beings also live within a very specific environment. We need the elements that occur naturally on our earth. Even when people live in cities, they are still part of nature even if they feel out of touch. You can explore your link to nature whenever you want by taking the time to experience what is there naturally.

Experiencing Your Part in Nature
Find a place outdoors on the ground, perhaps some soft grass where you can sit undisturbed to meditate. Close your eyes and relax for a few minutes. Let your breathing become comfortable and quiet. Notice how the ground supports you. Put your hands palm down on the ground and try to sense the mass under you. Feel the air on your skin. Notice how you breathe in the air and then expel it out again. Become aware of the exchange with nature that is always going on. Listen to the sounds. Even if you hear the sounds of traffic or people talking, do you also hear birds chirping? Allow yourself to experience how you are part of this scene—not separate from it but one with nature—one with Tao.

Cause in Nature

According to the great eighteenth-century philosopher Immanuel Kant, all change happens in synchrony with cause and effect. When people understand what the underlying causes are that bring something about, they believe they know what it is. For example, the Behavioral theory in behavioral psychology holds that all behavior is caused by stimuli from the environment. Therefore, behaviorists try to analyze the external factors that cause responses known as reflex reactions. Confucianism also believes in causes. Each "thing" is linked in a chain to the preceding "thing." Therefore, people can initiate a positive change at any point along the chain.

Taoism has a different explanation. When people take a Taoist perspective they recognize that things are not merely caused in sequence, from one to another. Instead, everything is what it is in relation to another thing. For this reason, you should not go outside of a thing to understand what it is. Searching for what came before as a possible cause of what comes after takes you away from what the thing is in relation to other things and events that lead to its relation to Tao.

Nature is more than cause and effect in one direction. The relationship among the five elements explains how nature is not unidirectional. The process is one of mutual influence, promoting, and restraining. Just as the cause leads to effect, effect leads backward to other conditions, to causes. The cycle is complex and continuous. Modern science is coming to similar understandings.

The Tao of Human Nature

Human beings are born with a mind and body that thinks and feels. Your thoughts and feelings help to attune you to your life, bringing you in synchrony with Tao.

Human babies know how to nurse from birth—no one needs to teach them. When they feel happy, they laugh. Psychologists call such inborn natural tendencies instincts, or conditioned reflexes. But the Taoists teach that these natural instincts can be more than just reflex tendencies. They give us an intuitive capacity to know a great deal about ourselves and our lives. We all have the ability to know what to do to find satisfaction. This ability is inbred in our nature through the mind we have all been given. Chuang-tzu said, "If a man follows the mind given him and makes it his teacher, then who can be without a teacher?" (Watson 1968, 18).

Cultivating Inner Nature

People are born with a nature that develops over time. By listening correctly to yourself, you can develop harmony with the nature around you by using your inborn abilities to sense, think, and feel. We often ignore the deeper sense of ourselves and our world by engaging attention on superficial matters. Chuang-tzu said, "Great understanding is broad and unhurried; little understanding is cramped and busy"

(Watson 1968, 37). Taoism encourages us away from the superficial and toward the deeper, more comprehensive sense of ourselves and our world. If you cultivate the root, flowers will grow of themselves.

Inward Glance I: Sensations

Lie on your back with your knees bent and feet flat on the floor. This allows your back to be completely relaxed. Let your mind scan your body and notice your body's sensations. Do your muscles feel tight? Which ones are tight and which ones are relaxed. Let your mind move around your body but do not try to change anything. Allow nature to take its course. Often tightness is an unnecessary clenching of muscles. If you become aware that you are tensing any areas, gently let go if this feels like the right thing to do, allow your muscles to find a comfortable relaxation.

Inward Glance II: Thoughts

Sit up and continue allowing your muscles to stay relaxed. Turn your attention to your thoughts. Follow the flow of your thoughts without influencing them. What are you thinking about? Do you flow from idea to idea, or are your thoughts clustered around a single concern? Notice the ideas and concerns but do not interfere. Simply try to be aware and allow your ideas to develop on their own.

Inward Glance III: Feelings

Intuitive feelings can also be a guide to deeper levels of the Tao. Sit with your eyes closed. Relax your breathing. What are you feeling? Don't force a response, simply wait for one to occur to you. Do you feel calm and quiet? As you sit there, perhaps you notice other feelings. Whatever you experience, allow your feelings to be.

When you take an inward glance at your sensations, thoughts, and feelings, you are listening to your inner nature. Trust that your inner nature is speaking to you. Take an inward glance from time to time through your day. Do not force anything—simply notice what is going on within. Over time you will get to know your deeper nature.

Sensing as Your Guide

You can attune to Tao with your senses, but the senses may mislead you, taking you away from the true Way. Lao-tzu points out how this happens and what to do about it.

> The clarity of seeing
> Is blinded by bright colors.
> The sharpness of hearing
> Is dulled by loud sounds.
> The keenness of tasting
> Is overcome by rich flavors.
> Indulging the senses
> Interferes with insight.
> Precious things
> Are distracting.
> —*Tao Te Ching* 12, Grigg 1995, 73

Most people have experienced the unpleasant effects of excessive stimuli. After too large a meal, we often feel sated and groggy. Indulging in excessive pleasures will inevitably lead to the opposite experience. Catering to the senses interferes with the Way. Unlike Buddhism, which advocates giving up craving entirely, Taoism takes a more moderate position, returning us to a natural balance.

Human beings have motivations, wishes, hopes, and desires that allow us to express who we are. But excessive expression of these human tendencies becomes artificial and leads us away from our true being. Thus Taoists do not recommend that we cut off all desires and sensations. Temper your desires and stay with the simple. By having and doing less, you experience and enjoy more.

The Uncarved Block

In sameness, knowing nothing
Not parted from their Power
In sameness, desiring nothing!
Call it, "the simple and unhewn."
—*Tao Te Ching*, Graham 1981, 20

The high point for humanity, according to Taoism, was when people lived side by side with the animals in nature. They lived simply and were fulfilled in all they did. "In the simple and unhewn the nature of the people is found" (Chuang-tzu in Graham 1981, 205).

The unhewn or uncarved block is a metaphor in Taoism, showing us the importance of a simple adjustment. But the Taoists are not advising people to just simplify their lives into nothing. Rather, by living as a close companion to nature, we are open to more creative potential.

Before a piece of wood is carved, it is filled with potential. It could become anything the woodcarver wants to make it. Thus it could be seen as having unlimited potential. But only in this primitive state does the uncarved block have such potential. Once the block is carved, it becomes only the one thing: the carving, with a finite shape and a definite meaning. As a finite something, the object undergoes the cycle of decay. People use it. With the passage of time, the luster of the surface fades. The cuts from the carver's knife become dull and eventually parts may break off, leaving the object marred and deformed. But for as long as the block remains uncarved, there are no expectations for it, no definitions, no distinctions. Whatever it becomes is what it is. The block remains One with Tao.

The lesson here is to be like the uncarved block. Do not limit your potential. By remaining open to everything, you can be spontaneous and free—two very important qualities for true happiness and for creativity.

Return to the Primitive

A sage said, "The richness of inner virtue is like an infant." Who does not start life as an infant? If we can clear away the stain of habits, we return to our primal innocence; the virtue of sages is simply this.

—Cleary 2000, 73

Taoism returns us to the primitive where we are closest to Tao. We have a long tradition of valuing the primitive in Western culture: the noble savage. The Taoist theme of reverence for the beginnings of things, for the virtue of simplicity, is fundamental to us. In the dialogue known as the "Meno," Plato showed that knowledge and understanding are innate; education is not adding something but, rather, remaining attuned to what is already potentially there. "Getting back to basics" is an expression we all know. Modern science has embraced Occam's Razor: the simplest, most fundamental explanation and theory is the best one. Taoism has held this for thousands of years. By truly understanding this principle, you can learn.

The uncarved block is the source of potential, wisdom, and creation. Its beginning is filled with positive potential, with unknown capacity. So Taoism encourages you to return to the beginnings, to the source of here and now. Then the wellspring of potential flows.

> When the Tao
> Is no longer followed,
> Propriety and virtue arise,
> Then comes knowledge.
> And then ingenuity.
> And finally cunning and hypocrisy.
> —*Tao Te Ching* 18, Grigg 1995, 82

When laws are imposed from the outside, they lead to lawlessness. Complex cultures take us away from our roots. People will be lawful naturally when they start from Tao. They will evolve of themselves if given the chance. Outer form and rules of conduct must be based in something deeper—the formless Tao. A house, for example, cannot exist if there is no empty space between the walls—we would have an almost two-dimensional object instead. Similarly, without the primitive, there can be no sophistication. Without a core, evolution is not possible. Your inner nature should come first; it is timeless, as yet uncreated, but implies what will be. Who you authentically are will always be more important than outer appearances.

So return to your formless inner essence, your uncarved block, to envision the future. The future is foreshadowed in the present moment. Inner resonance with Tao is the foundation for morality, achievement, and accomplishment.

Natural Talents

Taoists believe that each person has certain talents even though some people may not recognize what these talents are. Some people are very aware of what they excel in and express their talents from an early age, developing them to their fullest. They feel a deep inner satisfaction from following their inner nature.

But other people are not as sure about their aptitudes, so they choose to get direction from external sources. These choices may lead away from true inner nature. Undeveloped talents go untapped and remain dormant within, waiting to be discovered. These people might feel somewhat unfulfilled, compelled, or unhappy without quite knowing why. Taoism guides you back to your own human nature and shows you how to follow it. The exercise that follows will help you to attune to your true inner nature, the source of Tao within.

Discovering Your Natural Talents Exercise

Think back on your youth. What did you like to do when you played as a young child? Did you love puzzles? Were you happiest riding a bike or running outdoors? Or did you pass your time reading or coloring? Some children enjoy doing magic tricks, others like building blocks. You may not have thought about these interests in a long time.

When you remember something you enjoyed doing, try to do it now. Of course, you might do it in a more adult way—for example, if you enjoyed building blocks, perhaps you would like to construct something in another medium, wood, perhaps, or cloth, or perhaps a virtual construction such as 3-D modeling. If you enjoyed running as a child, perhaps you would like jogging now. Taoism would predict that by returning to your early, spontaneous impulse toward activity you will discover your natural hidden talents.

Returning to the Uncarved Block

Sit in meditation. Close your eyes and relax your body. Think back to when you were very young, before you became an adult. Can you reexperience your youthful innocence, before you decided what you wanted to do with your life, when summer seemed endless and the world immense? Return to your roots and you will find the essence.

Wu-Wei

Accomplish More by Doing Less

Wriggling about, growing stiff, and getting stuck in shallow, meaninglessness—that is the fate of "doers." But life does nothing and yet nothing is undone. For by the relaxing and allowing itself to be permeated by Tao, life develops limitlessly and reaches into the mysterious cosmic depth.

—Wilhelm 1990, 85

Taoism has a unique perspective on how to succeed in everything you do in life. They call it *wu-wei,* the way of nonaction. When you incorporate wu-wei into your life, everything becomes easier and more natural. Things seem to happen of themselves. The key is to learn how to set forces of nature in motion to help you accomplish without effort.

Lao-tzu shows how important nonaction is to life. Numerous passages in the *Tao Te Ching* are devoted to encouraging wu-wei in many different contexts. Here are but a few examples:

Tao invariably takes no action and
yet there is nothing left undone.
　　—*Tao Te Ching* 37, Chan 1963, 158

Act without action
Do without ado.
　　—*Tao Te Ching* 63, Chan 1963, 169

D. T. Suzuki was a famous Zen Buddhist who brought Eastern philosophies to the West by doing some of the earliest translations of oriental classics into English. Although most of his work was in the area of
Zen and Buddhism, one of his first translations was the *Tao Te Ching*.
Suzuki translated "wei" as meaning "to do something," but also to act,
like being on a stage or "to make a show, to show off, to pose, to
parade oneself." "Wu" is a negation that means "lacking in, nonexistent,
without." Wu refers to absence. So Suzuki translated wu-wei as nonact
(Suzuki & Carus 1974, 16). Wu-wei can be interpreted as acting without ado, or acting without falseness: being true and sincere to the
deeper essence. Wu-wei can also mean taking no action that is contrary to nature. Don't interfere. Instead, attune yourself to what is happening and go with it.

Nonaction

The first step on the way to Tao is to be in harmony with, not in
rebellion against the fundamental laws of the universe.
　　　　　　　　　　　　　—Chuang-tzu in Waley 1958, 55

Wu-wei is the logical consequence of Taoist philosophy. Everything is
always flowing according to its cycles. Life progresses its own way. We
are born, we live, and we die. Without any effort, day turns to night,
spring becomes summer, acorns grow into trees, and children mature
into adults. These cycles and patterns are inevitable. Wu-wei teaches

that if you want to accomplish anything in life, the best way is to align yourself with these natural forces. The current flows downstream, so if you want to travel efficiently and well, you would be wise to ride with the current, not against it.

Sometimes going with the flow doesn't seem like the correct thing to do, even though it is. A simple example is clearly experienced if a car skids on a slippery road. Often, the first impulse is to brake and turn the steering wheel in the opposite direction to counterbalance the force. But if the skid is opposed, the car will spin faster. The best way to regain control is to steer in the direction of the skid and then to gently steer out of it. Turning the wheel with the skid allows the car to right itself; similarly, following the flow puts you back in control.

When you take no action that is contrary to the natural flow of your life, you gain a certain power that the Taoists call Te. Then, all the forces of nature work in your favor and nothing stops your progress (see Lesson Ten). Let things act by themselves and they will do what they do. Then everything works out as it should.

Living Wu-wei

How do you do without doing? This skill can be developed using meditation. By exploring the very roots of action you can begin to let go of doing and discover your deeper nature, in tune with Tao.

Standing and sitting are basic human actions that seem natural to our being. But many people interfere with their natural, inborn ability to do these things effortlessly. While growing up, people may have told you to "Sit up straight" or "Keep your head up." Sometimes tall people take on a hunch to appear shorter, or short people arch to look taller. These types of habits come from external input that interferes with the natural ability to sit and stand. If you pay attention, you may be surprised to discover all the ways that you make standing and sitting exhausting and stressful. By following the Tao of standing, you can reclaim your inborn capacity and let gravity do the work.

Exercise I: Letting Go

Stand up and close your eyes. Notice how you are standing but don't change anything yet. Do you put more weight on one foot than the other? Are your shoulders hunched? Is your head forward or toward one side of your body? Do you hold yourself upright by arching your back? Pay attention to any tightness you feel.

Feel your feet on the floor. Do they push against the floor or can you allow your feet to relax to the floor, taking the support that is given. Feel your legs. Are they tight, knees locked? Try letting them be naturally straight without forcing. Is your back tight, perhaps arched or slumped? Relax gently. Do your arms hang at your side or are they forward from hunched shoulders or back from thrusting your chest forward? Find what feels like a natural position for your arms and allow them to hang naturally. Can you let go of any unnatural pushing or pulling?

Exercise II: Effortless Standing

Take your shoes off and stand with your feet approximately shoulder-width apart, arms hanging comfortably at your sides. Close your eyes. Scan your body with your mind and notice any tightness. If possible, relax and then shift very gently and slowly, forward and back. As you shift forward feel your weight move over your toes. Can you feel the front of your body tightening? Now shift your weight back, over your heels. Do you feel the back of your body tightening to compensate? What else do you notice? Gently rock back and forth, making smaller and smaller movements until you feel a center point where all your muscles are most relaxed. You are now aligned with gravity and standing takes the least effort.

Now, shift from side to side, first over the left foot, then over the right. Feel how, as you leave the center, your muscles tighten and standing becomes more difficult, but when you are directly in the center again, standing feels effortless. Rock gently from side to side until you find your center and you are equally balanced between each foot. Take a few moments to enjoy balanced, effortless standing.

Allowing Sitting

Sit cross-legged on the floor. If you can't sit comfortably cross-legged, sit with your legs slightly apart, knees bent, with your arms around your knees. Close your eyes. Hold your head upright so that your back is fairly straight. Do not strain to be straight but do not slouch either. You should feel a free flow of air as you breathe gently in and out. Allow your rib cage to move as you breathe. Pay attention to your body sensations. Do you feel comfortable or are you fighting to keep upright? Does your breathing feel constricted? Can you let go of effort, or do you need to tense a little? Try stretching your midsection slightly. Does this open the air passages? If so, perhaps you have been slumping forward without realizing it. Be comfortable. Accept your posture as it is most comfortable and let it be.

Effortless Chair Sitting

Much of our daily sitting is done in chairs, where we are not so much sitting in chairs as we are using up energy pushing on them. This exercise will help you obtain support from a chair while continuing to be aligned with gravity for effortless sitting.

Use a desk or dining chair. Stand with your back facing the chair. Pay attention as you slowly lower yourself into the chair. Do you feel as though you are dropping into the chair or does your body lower gracefully? Can you continue to remain balanced as you descend? Once in the chair, how do you sit? Do you lean against the chair back? Does your back sag or are you more comfortable fairly upright? Do your feet rest on the floor or are they pushing against it? Do you allow the chair to hold you or are you holding yourself in the chair?

Practice several times standing up and sitting down slowly, with awareness. Try to let go of any actions that prevent you from sitting comfortably and taking support from the chair.

Meditations for Nonaction

Not-Doing Meditation

To turn toward Tao, lessen your conscious experience until you arrive at nonaction. Find a quiet place where you can be undisturbed for a time. You can begin with as little as one minute, and gradually increase the time up to fifteen or so. Sit quietly and close your eyes. Let your thoughts slow by allowing them to flow without any interference. At first you might think of all the things you should be doing—perhaps what you have to do later or what you did earlier—but try not to dwell on them. Simply let these thoughts be as you continue to sit quietly and do nothing. If you find yourself carried away by a thought, gently bring yourself back to doing nothing. With practice, you will find that you can be comfortable doing nothing. Practice this meditation at different times. You may be surprised how a short period of not-doing can have a positive, lasting effect throughout your busy day.

Meditative Action

Once you feel some progress with the previous meditations, try applying nonaction to an activity. This might seem like a contradiction, to act without acting, but you may be surprised at how much action is wasted effort. When you approach your actions the Taoist way, you can accomplish things with ease and have energy left over!

Start small, with a simple activity, such as washing the dishes or washing the car. Meditate for a moment to quiet yourself, then begin. Try to let the soap and the sponge help you accomplish your task by using the natural capacity of soap to dissolve and the natural capacity of the sponge to absorb. Notice if you are tensing your muscles, hunching your back, or tightening your shoulders. How are you standing? Focus your attention on the task but don't think anything about it. Try not to judge whether it is easy or difficult, going quickly or slowly. Also, do not worry about whether you like or dislike the task. Simply do it. Minimize your effort and you will be surprised how easily you achieve your goal.

No-Knowledge

If only human beings
did not need to always be right
Think of how seldom
people would fight.
We'd get along better
with a lot less defenses
And feel quite secure
without high walls and fences.
We'd accept each other more
and respect each other's needs
We'd feel our inner oneness
Beyond gender, race, age, or creed.
                    —C. Alexander Simpkins

The idea of wu-wei also applies to knowledge and learning. We in the West believe that a well-educated person has accumulated a great deal of knowledge. The more a person knows, the wiser he or she is. But Taoism has a very different idea about what makes a person wise.

Accumulating knowledge simply adds something that is external to our true nature. Like piling on one heavy weight after another, this kind of outer knowledge bogs us down and stands in the way of inner wisdom. Facts and theories we learn are simply man-made labels and constructs. Taoists advise people to cast off knowledge.

Throw out all convention, saintliness, and knowledge. They are all illusions, nothing but names invented by men and then held in high esteem.

—Chuang-tzu in Watson 1968, 90

Deeper wisdom is obscured by all the facts we accumulate about a topic. For example, when learning a profession, students go through extensive schooling that teaches everything that is known within the field. They study and memorize the many theories that have come to be accepted over the years as true. If they are learning a science, research is cited as evidence for each theory. Knowledge about what is known becomes the student's orientation for viewing the world. Taoists believe this orientation blocks perception. Like wearing distorting glasses, the many theories and concepts obscure perceiving what is really there.

Sometimes the most inventive solutions come when you can step away from what is known. The famed hypnotherapist Milton Erickson had a client who was not progressing. Erickson tried many techniques and considered numerous theories about the patient's problem, all without success. Before the next session, he hypnotized himself to forget everything he knew about this patient, as if he were meeting him for the first time. Experiencing the patient directly without his theories and ideas to get in the way, Erickson was able to help him.

Relativity

As people accumulate knowledge, they form opinions. From the perspective of their opinions, they contend with other views. But Chuang-tzu questioned the importance of such arguing. He asked, if I win an argument, does that mean I'm right and you're wrong? Or if you win, does that make me wrong? Or are we both right and both wrong? Arguments are always waged from a relativistic point of view. Each side is narrow and doesn't encompass the whole. Our ideas of right and wrong are always based on our finite point of view. The Taoist understands that there can be no "right" without the idea of "wrong." In fact, as soon as you take a position, the opposite is also created. Lao-tzu explained this in Chapter 2 of the *Tao Te Ching*:

> If all people of the world know that beauty is beauty, there is
> then already ugliness. If all people of the world know that good
> is good, there is then already evil. (Fung Yu-lan 1966, 101)

No object in the world is really long or short. These terms have meaning only in comparison to a standard, and standards are always relative. If we view the world from a relative basis, we are doomed to limited and mistaken understandings. Chuang-tzu described an enormous bird like an eagle whose name is P'eng. This bird traveled across the earth, flying up to ninety thousand miles. A little dove heard about the long and high travels of the P'eng and laughed at this. "When I try to fly, I can go as high as the elm tree and as far as I need to go. If you tried to travel ninety thousand miles, you would need provisions for three months! What a waste of effort." From his small perspective, the dove could not fathom the vast perspective of the P'eng. And the P'eng would miss the small details discerned by the dove. Neither perspective would be real or understandable to the other because both are locked into their own limited perception.

Tao Transcends

Whenever you add anything, it takes you away from Tao. Accumulating knowledge leads you away from what is already there, your inner sense of how things are. Take no position and you free your mind to be able to understand the larger perspective of Tao.

When you follow the way of wu-wei you are not pushed and pulled by man-made forces of society. Your inner sense guides you. Inner intuition is your direct link to the greater Tao. Attune to your simple self, the deeper you, and you will know Tao.

Using No-Knowledge to Truly Know Exercise

No-knowledge begins as a state of mind, an approach to everyday life. To experiment with this idea, take all of your philosophies, opinions, and beliefs and temporarily set them aside. This exercise is very similar to the method used by the famous Western philosopher René Descartes when he doubted everything he could to arrive at the one thing he was certain of: "I think therefore I am." Taoists compare this state of mind to an infant. Infants feel and perceive, but they do not have any abstract theories or constructs. Become aware of what actually is without having any concepts about it.

Look around your house. What do you really perceive? For example, what do you feel as you touch the top of your table? Do you feel coolness, warmth, smoothness? Can you forget the names and labels for things and simply experience what is there?

Let go of judgments as well. For example, when you look around, don't judge whether the room is clean or messy—simply experience. See what you see, hear what you hear, feel what you feel and nothing more. At first your mind will race on with thoughts as usual. But keep returning to your direct experiencing whenever you can.

No-Thought Meditation

Pick a time when you are relaxed or perhaps only a bit tired, so that your thoughts are already slowed down. Find a comfortable place to sit quietly. Notice the moments between thoughts when you spontaneously think about nothing. Invite your mind to extend these moments without thought, and wait. Try not to interfere. You don't have to do anything or think anything in particular. Simply allow your natural abilities to emerge.

Take a few minutes during your day to sit down and allow yourself to think of nothing. Be curious and interested in the process as you discover the benefits of wordless, idealess experiencing.

Visualizing to Stillness Meditation

The usefulness of a bowl is in its emptiness, so by letting your mind become empty, you open the door to all the potential benefits of wu-wei.

Visualization can be a useful tool for meditation, to help give you an experience of a calm, clear mind. The later Taoist movements used the power of visualization extensively to help them extend their capacities. Find a comfortable place to sit or lie down. Close your eyes. Picture a peaceful vista—grassy, rolling hills; a calm lake; or a quiet forest. You may want to remember a place you enjoyed visiting or create one. All is quiet, still. In fact, it is so quiet that you can almost hear your own heartbeat. Your muscles relax a bit, effortlessly. The colors are soothing; the breeze is soft. As you imagine this peaceful scene, your thoughts slow down, leaving an experience of calm and stillness. Do not do anything other than enjoy the scene.

Reflection in the Mirror Mind

Let your mind be like a mirror, calm and clear. Mirror your surroundings. This means allowing yourself to pick up any environmental stimuli. You might hear birds sing or traffic go by, feel a breeze, the warmth of a summer day. Be centered in the moment, aware, and in touch. Then you can intuitively know without knowing.

Yin and Yang

Accepting and Integrating Opposites

Inside and outside
They need each other
No black without white
No sister without brother.
We have no tomorrow
Without today
Speech is not possible
Without something to say.
There are no wise ones
Without the fools.
The nature of life
Is expressed in the dual.

—C. Alexander Simpkins

From the One Comes Everything

Taoism evolved in three stages. In the beginning was Tao. The first
humans looked up to the heavens, then down to the earth. They rec-

ognized the will of heaven and its expression on the earth. Then a boundary, the horizon, gradually appeared. Thus, the Tao of heaven and the Tao of earth emerged. Finally, the Tao of humanity issued forth. A horizontal line has often been used to symbolize this division, and so the sense of order in the universe gradually formed in the mind of primitive humanity.

The saying from the *Tao Te Ching* explains this: From the Tao, One; from One, two; from two, three, and then the universe of infinite numbers of things. The sequence of action is to begin with Tao, then you will always understand the beginning and end. Tao is the origin, the source, before creation.

Scientists think of the world and its forces in numbers: one and zero. One and zero are the basis for computers. But we can also think of one and zero as universe and nothingness.

The underlying unity of logic is the basis of all knowledge. We know things by comparing them to their opposite, nonthings. The universe of things must be compared with the universe of nonthings. This logic is the method of difference by comparison. For example, we know a sheep by comparing it to a creature that is not a sheep. How do they differ? The Greek philosophers Aristotle and Plato believed that logic comes first; the Way follows from logic. Therefore, Taoist logic, of yin and yang, is similar to the fundamental logic of Aristotle, turned around. For Taoism, the Way comes first and logic follows the Way.

Contrast leads to dissolution. Remove contrast, and harmony results. Differences combine to form Tao. All sound thinking begins with viewing the universe of things and classes of things as a function of that unity. And unity is a function of a higher or larger unity that synthesizes all distinctions. Tao is the synthesis beyond yin and yang—zero.

Experiencing the Contrast of Yin and Yang

We use yin and yang in perception constantly. For example, our visual receptors from the eye to the brain discern patterns of objects by contrast. We have sensory receptors that react to differences in our retinas. One type of receptor is sensitive to stimulation "on center," contrasting with the surrounding or off-center periphery. We see things because of the contrast between the on-center and off-center firing of neurons.

Yin-Yang Perception Exercise I
Yin and yang are built into how we perceive things. You can experience this for yourself with this simple exercise. Look at a light for a few minutes, then shut your eyes. You will see a dark image that takes on the shape of the light you saw.

Yin-Yang Perception Exercise II
You will also perceive the opposite when you look at a color. Tape a red square of paper to a white wall. Look at it for a few minutes and then shut your eyes. The image of a green square will appear. Visual receptors for red are in balance with visual receptors for the opposite color, green. When we exhaust the red receptors, green ones are activated until the balance is restored. Our visual system has its own yin-yang balance always interacting to help us see our world.

Qualities of Yin and Yang

Chinese philosophy has given yin and yang certain characteristics that define and distinguish them. Yang is associated with the active male and heaven. It is white, high, and expanding. Yang also refers to the immaterial and energy. As an element, yang is fire and is hot.

Yin is associated with the female, passive, and interior. It is dark in color, cold in temperature, and moving down. Its element is water, which, as the *Tao Te Ching* states, is always seeking the low. Yin is linked to the material—the earth and matter. Taoism often favors yin over yang, believing that from the lower comes the higher, but both will eventually manifest through the cycles of life.

The divisions are subtle because within most yin there is always some degree of yang, and within most yang some yin: There is always yang and yin, ever dividing infinitely. Pure qualities only exist for a fleeting moment, such as at midnight. Inevitably the wheel of time turns and it is 12:01. The cycle flows continuously.

	Yin		Yang	
Yin	Yang	Yang	Yin
Yin Yang	Yin Yang	Yin Yang	Yin Yang

Yin-Yang Manifests in the World

Yin and yang are expressed in every facet of living, our inner being and the outer world. Chinese theory explains how yin and yang integrate with time and space. The four seasons and times of day are various degrees of yin and yang.

Tao-Unity
Yin - - Yang

yang	yin	yin	yang
within	within	within	within
yang	yang	yin	yin
———	———	— —	— —
———	— —	— —	———
summer	autumn	winter	spring
noon	sunset	midnight	sunrise

At any point in the cycles of time we can sense certain qualities that distinguish it. For example, in the middle of winter at midnight, we would expect it to be cold, dark, and quiet—yin qualities. At noon in the middle of summer, things tend to be bright, warm, and active, the qualities of yang.

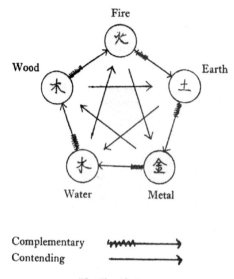

Fire

Wood

Earth

Water

Metal

| Complementary | |
| Contending | |

The Five Elements

The Five-Element Theory

These yin-yang relationships are also intertwined within the universe: heaven (yang) and earth (yin). The universe is further divided into five fundamental elements: earth, wind, metal, fire, and water.

The five elements are always transforming each other, just as yin and yang are always changing into each other. Each element restrains or overcomes another element while each element also promotes another element. For some examples on the restraining side: fire consumes wood, water will put out a fire, dams can be built with earth to prevent flooding (earth consumes water), metals are softened by fire (fire consumes metal), an ax can cut down a tree (metal overcomes wood). Examples of how elements promote each other: water helps trees to grow (water promotes wood), wood burns to ashes (fire promotes earth).

Pa Kua Hexagram

Pa Kua, the Trigrams

Yin and yang are expanded from pairs into trigrams of three. The combinations of three lines altogether are known as the pa kua. There are eight combinations of three. Feng shui, chi kung, and a martial art known as pa kua draw heavily on the pa kua diagram as their guide.

The two pure trigrams are Ch'ien and K'un. Ch'ien is the most yang trigram, the archetype of male—strong, hard, and white. K'un is the most yin trigram, symbolizing the mother, or female—weak, soft, and dark.

These two trigrams combine together to form sixty-four hexagrams. Together, these sixty-four hexagrams are the guidelines for interpretation in the *I Ching*.

Using Yin and Yang

Taoism encourages you to view circumstances from a broad perspective, with attention to contrast and difference, in order to choose wisely. Yin and yang come from Tao, beginning as passive, feminine, relaxed. These qualities are closest to Tao. Soft overcomes hard. So let be, wait, facilitate, seek the balance of opposites. But yin and yang are complementary. Don't engage in action without recognizing that the opposite will follow as a cyclic counterpart. Action leads to consequence, yin evokes yang: change and transformation are continuous.

Opening Yourself to Both Sides Exercise
Imagine a situation as the opposite. For example, imagine that a difficulty is not a difficulty, that it is an advantage. What thoughts do you have about it when you think of it as the opposite?

Reversal

Dynamic interplay comes about when material forces evolve. A line leads to something above and something below, which polarizes into opposites that lead to the reverse. Night always becomes day, and day reverts to night again. A circle has a center and a circumference: inside the circle and outside the circle. The cycle of life flows from being to nonbeing, and back to being. Define an object and you also define what it is not. Don't take sides quickly, because you know that reversion takes effect. The exercise that follows will help you make sense of this Taoist idea of change and show you how to make change a resource for you.

Don't Take Sides Exercise
Sit quietly for a few minutes and clear your mind. Think of a one-sided situation, perhaps something that you have always done a certain way. Think about the yin and yang and how things always flow from one to the other. This may stretch your imagination a bit, especially if you are set on one way. Try to genuinely experience the change.

Synthesis

The dynamic interplay of yin and yang leads to a synthesis at a higher level. Since the synthesis includes them both, they are linked, like heads and tails on a coin—even though there are two sides, they are both part of the same coin.

Carl Jung was a famous psychoanalyst who was one of the first in the West to integrate Eastern philosophy into his approach. He showed that yin and yang polarities are an integral part of deep psychotherapy. We want to unify, to become whole, to balance the opposite polarities of our personality. By allowing both sides of an inner or outer conflict to speak and be heard, synthesis becomes possible. Just letting both sides shout it out does not resolve differences, nor does it make resolution necessarily possible in and of itself. Both sides must be willing to listen.

Accepting All of You

You can recognize the continual interplay of opposites within you and accept both sides. Both are inevitable. The reason people don't notice the opposite is that they have a preference for one side over the other. For example, most people would say that they don't like their angry, aggressive side and would prefer to be only their caring, affectionate side. But by throwing out aggression we may lose the ability to be assertive, a useful quality of aggression. Instead, it can be transformed, brought into balance through caring and affection, so that anger is constructive and firm rather than destructive and aggressive. By accepting, you can transform.

Like water, the Tao seeks low places. It does not reject the lowest, the worst, the ugliest. Chuang-tzu explains why:

> When men do not lose sight of what is out of sight but do lose sight of what is in plain sight, we may speak of "the oversight which is seeing things as they are." (Graham 1981, 80)

People say "I don't like this person because he is ugly." They dislike this and like that for some reason. But judgments of good and bad, like and dislike come from a limited perspective. People create the relativistic sphere of social convention, but the Tao transcends such limits. After we understand yin and yang, we recognize that even the most ugly, most deformed creature has the capacity for the greatest beauty. Through the Tao, all distinctions dissolve into Oneness, a harmony that is just as it should be.

People often apply this same logic to themselves. They like this trait in themselves and dislike that one. But when we reject a part of our inner self, we move away from the Path. We lose Tao and become unbalanced. Even though it may seem contrary to logic to accept something about yourself that you do not like, this is the first step to overcoming it. For example, we had a self-critical client. She felt that she was not a very nice person. She would lash out at her partner without provocation. But she found that the more she tried to control her reactions, the meaner she became. She thought of herself as "ugly" when she acted that way.

She expected therapy to help her curtail her "ugly" side. But to her surprise we encouraged a Taoist approach. "Accept your negative qualities," we told her. "They are just as much a part of you as the beautiful ones." She thought about this and began to consider how hidden within these negative behaviors were positive qualities only partially expressed. Her mean side was strong and assertive. She was struggling with being too submissive at times. This led to her anger with others. Some of her ability to be assertive was bound up in this struggle against herself. By accepting her "ugly" side, she began to change. At the close of therapy, she did not behave with meanness and was able to be strong when appropriate.

Exercise in Self-acceptance

You can integrate the Taoist idea of not making distinctions and judgments that take you away from the larger perspective of Tao by thinking about your distinctions and judgments of yourself.

Think about your own qualities. Do you have some behavior that you do not like about yourself and are trying to stop? Do you criticize yourself about it? Consider it, instead, from the broader perspective of Tao. What is the polar opposite of this trait? Try to find the positive in this opposite. What are your positive intentions before you become negative? Find a more constructive perspective, one that allows both sides to be. This adjustment moves you closer to Tao.

Chi

Activate Your Energy

Dao [Tao] generates the One
The One generates the Two
The Two generates the Three,
The Three generates all things
All things have darkness at their back
and strive towards the light,
and the flowing power gives them harmony.
—*Tao Te Ching* 42, Wilhelm 1990, 46

From Tao comes yin and yang. The ancient Chinese believed that with the division of yin and yang, yin energy flowed upward to form the heavens and yang energy flowed downward to form the earth. From the dynamic interaction between yin and yang, chi flows. Chi is manifested in every area of living, from our inner health and vitality to the outer environment and the greater world.

When chi flows freely, everything works as it should; when chi is blocked, problems develop. The Chinese have developed methods to foster chi's flow in all the vital areas of living: for vitality and long life through chi kung and Inner Alchemy; for health through Eastern medicine; for comfortable, prosperous living through Outer Alchemy and Feng Shui; and for self-defense and higher development through the martial arts.

Chi Is Both Matter and Energy

The concept of chi is ancient and transcends time and place. The word *chi* corresponds to the Greek word *pneuma* and the Sanskrit word *prana*, meaning breath, respiration, wind, and vital spirit, soul. Everything in the universe, both inert and active, is part of the vast sea of chi.

Everything is chi, both solid matter and energy. Taoists don't make a clear distinction between matter and energy or between the material and the spiritual, and this is reflected in how chi is defined. Modern physicists might agree to an extent, because on the molecular level all matter in our universe is comprised of subatomic particles: positive, negative, and neutral energy interacting together.

Western philosophers have struggled with the idea of materialism versus spiritualism, a separation of mind and body that has permeated Western thinking. Some modern scientists have tried to resolve this dualism by reducing everything spiritual to the material level. To material theorists, the mind is only a phenomenon, a reflection of the brain's structure. If we understand all the parts of the brain, we will then understand the mind.

But early-twentieth-century French philosopher Henri Bergson conceived of material and spiritual as an intimately intertwined unity, which is similar to Taoism. He called the nonmaterial life force the "elan vital," the process of existence. This life force is not static or material, but it is related to the material. Bergson offered a way of thinking about the relationship that is helpful for understanding chi's quality of being both energy and material at the same time:

A very small element of a curve is very near to being a straight line. In the limit it may be termed a part of the straight line, as you please, for in each of its points a curve coincides with its tangent. So likewise, "vitality" is tangent at any and every point to physical and chemical forces, but such points are, in fact, only views taken by a mind which imagines stops at various moments of movement that generates the curve. In reality, life is no more made up of physico-chemical elements than a curve is composed of straight lines. (Bergson in Durant 1968, 455)

Chi manifests itself in so many ways in our world that it serves as a good example of how the nonmaterial and material are actually two sides of the same coin—they are One. Chi is nonmaterial, an energy somewhat like electricity that cannot be seen under a microscope, yet without it, material things would not be what they are. Chi is manifested throughout the material world, giving living things the vitality and spirit that makes them alive. Chi reveals the view that everything and everyone is part of a universal unity.

Chi Kung

Being flexible and relaxed allows chi to flow smoothly. But you can do more to cultivate your chi. Everyone is born with a certain amount of energy. Chi kung is a Chinese art that helps people to work with their given lot of energy to enhance it. Originally begun as a search for immortality, chi kung has developed in modern times into a set of meditations and movements to raise, enhance, and direct chi energy for positive use.

"Kung" means cultivating, working with, or developing and thus chi kung is a practice of cultivating chi. When you use these methods, you become aware of your chi energy as it flows through your body. Along with this awareness comes the ability to invigorate or calm yourself at will, a useful skill! Chi kung is also prescribed as part of

Eastern medicine, to help in treatment (see Lesson Six). Since a problem in energy flow is the basis for illness, chi kung may help with illness by restoring the flow of energy. Chi kung also overlaps with martial arts, where chi development is integral to the training (see Lesson Seven).

Cultivating chi involves sensitizing to a different aspect of functioning. We are very practiced at knowing what we are doing, where we are going, and what we are thinking. But sensing energy is only done in a vague, nonspecific manner: We feel energetic or tired, but the subtleties are missed. Chi kung opens perception to this important dimension of functioning. By becoming aware of your energy flow you will gain ability to work with your energy. When stressed and tense you will be able to unwind; when tired you will be able to invigorate yourself. According to chi kung theory, if you learn how to develop and direct your chi, you will have the foundation for much greater health and well-being (Gasgoigne 1997, 67).

The chi kung exercises that follow will help you to attune to your optimum energy level of functioning and then to use it for your benefit, depending on what you feel is needed. Chi kung gives you more control. If you have discomfort or difficulty performing these exercises, stop doing them and consult a qualified chi kung instructor.

Wei Dan and Nei Dan

Chi kung has two broad categories of practice that affect the flow of internal energy: Wei Dan and Nei Dan. Both can help you to raise your chi and then enhance and circulate it through your body. Both are thought to add vitality and longevity, but they do so using different methods.

Wei Dan increases chi by stimulating one area. The chi builds up in that area and then spills over through the meridians. Alchemical Taoists thought of this energy as being an elixir that nourishes and vitalizes the whole body, a healing medicine.

Nei Dan begins by generating chi in the energy center located in the lower abdomen. Then, using focused attention, chi is guided around the body through the two major vessels called the Conception Vessel and the Governor Vessel (see Lesson Seven for more about these vessels and the meridians). Circulating chi adds vitality and enhances well-being.

Wei Dan

Preliminary Wei Dan Exercise: Feeling Chi
Clap your hands together for fifteen seconds. Then close your eyes and feel the sensation in your hands. This is the chi energy that spontaneously goes to your palms because of the clapping. The tingling sensation is created by raising the energy level in your palms.

Developing Awareness of Chi
The previous exercise gave you a feeling of chi, but the true art of working with chi is subtler and involves using your mind. Mind and body are One, so when you focus your attention on an area of your body, your energy will tend to flow there.

Sit in a quiet place with your hands resting on your knees. Focus all your attention on the palms of your hands. Feel how warm they are and whether they seem heavy or light. Keep your attention focused on your hands. After a few minutes, do you begin to notice some tingling in your fingertips? Or do you feel a slight warming? Your chi is now flowing into your hands.

Experiment with other areas of focus. For example, focus your attention on your feet. Does some warmth or tingling develop there? Eventually you will feel a response in your body as soon as you begin to focus your attention. With practice, directing your chi will get easier.

Moving Wei Dan: Eight Pieces of Brocade
Wei Dan is traditionally performed by doing sets of movements that involve tensing and relaxing muscles. When doing Wei Dan you should

Chi

be relaxed and calm. Before you start, do one of the exercises given in the book to clear your mind of distraction and relax your body.

When you feel ready, try this series of traditional Wei Dan exercises known as the Eight Pieces of Brocade. These exercises date back to the Sung dynasty (A.D. 960–1279) in China. Brocade is a cloth with finely woven patterns of great beauty and value. These gentle exercises are beautiful patterns that have value for enhancing health and well-being.

Stand quietly for a few minutes. Let your breathing become calm and natural. Keep your back relatively straight. Perform the movements slowly, keeping your body relaxed. Repeat each piece three to five times and then proceed to the next one. Continue until you have done all eight.

These eight exercises, performed in sequence, activate the entire body. Be sure to keep your attention fully focused on the movement, as the mind is an important component for raising your chi. You will begin to feel a slight change in energy, experienced as warmth or tingling.

Piece One (Figures 1 and 2): Stand with your feet shoulder-width apart, hands dropped straight down at your sides. Exhaling, rotate your head to the left without straining. Keep the rest of your body still. Inhale as you bring your head back to face front, then exhale again as you turn your head to the right. Finally inhale while you turn to face front.

Piece Two (Figures 3–5): Bend your arms at the elbow, with backs of hand facing down. Intertwine your fingers together. Keeping your fingers intertwined, straighten your elbows pushing your hands in front of you with palms facing out, and then carefully swing your arms up and over your head as you exhale. As you inhale, bring your hands back down in front of your body. Return to the position with arms bent at the elbows.

Piece Three (Figures 6 and 7): With hands palm up in front of your body and elbows bent, unclasp your hands but leave the fingertips touching. As you exhale, move your left hand up over your head with your palm facing up as you simultaneously move your right hand down in front, palm down. As you inhale, return your hands to their original position. Then exhale as you reverse, raising the right hand overhead palm up and the left hand down palm down.

Piece Four (Figures 8–10): Begin with your fists held at your waist, palms facing up. While you inhale, step to the left into a slightly wider stance, known in martial arts as horse stance. Let your knees bend slightly. Exhale and turn your body to the left, extend and cross your arms in front of you. Exhale and open your left hand, palm facing away from you, as you draw your right hand back to your chest, as if drawing a bow. As you inhale, return to face front with both fists at your waist and the left foot drawn back in to shoulder width (the starting position). Now pivot to the right and repeat the pattern as you exhale, stepping out to the right, extending both hands to the right, and pulling back the bow. Turn back to face front while inhaling.

Piece Five (Figures 11 and 12): Step to the left into horse stance. Let your hands rest on your thighs. Exhale and lean to the left without raising your feet. Inhale as you return to center. Exhale while you lean to the right. Inhale as you return to center.

Piece Six (Figures 13 and 14): Bring your legs back to shoulder-width apart. Raise your hands, palms up, fingers touching as in Piece Three. Gently stretch forward as you exhale, and try to place your palms on the floor. As flexibility increases you will be able to touch the floor with your palms; don't try to go further than is comfortable. Inhale and slowly return to standing.

Piece Seven (Figures 15 and 16): From the horse stance position with fists at your sides, exhale as you slowly punch to the left with the left fist—your knuckles should be facing upward. Turn your head to the left as you punch. Return to the original position as you inhale, then punch to the right as you exhale, and return to center.

Piece Eight (Figure 17): For the final piece, stand with your feet together, hands at your sides. Keeping your legs straight, raise up on your toes while exhaling. Lower your heels slowly as you inhale.

Figure 1

Figure 2

Figure 3

Figure 4

Tao in Ten

Figure 5

Figure 6

Figure 7

Figure 8

Figure 9

Figure 10

Figure 11

Figure 12

Figure 13

Figure 14

Figure 15

Figure 16

Figure 17

Stationary Wei Dan: Mind Leads the Chi

Wei Dan can be performed by sitting quietly and imagining the motions without actually performing them. In this way, you move the chi to the areas more subtly. Once you are very familiar with the Eight Pieces of Brocade, try sitting quietly and imagine yourself doing the exercises. Do not move your body; simply picture yourself doing them. This will not only circulate chi, it will also help you improve how you actually perform the exercises when you do them again. This meditation can be done with any physical activity—martial arts, dance, tennis, weight lifting—and, in fact, is done by many great athletes prior to competition.

Nei Dan

Nei Dan, like Wei Dan has its roots in alchemical Taoism. The outer alchemical process of heating a cauldron to melt elements that would be drunk as elixirs for health and longevity was reinterpreted more wisely as a symbolic, internal transformation of spiritual elements to bring about health-giving effects.

Focus on Breathing

Chi has been thought of as the breath of life. By focusing on your breathing you can raise your energy and help ready yourself for the other Nei Dan methods.

Begin by sitting comfortably, either on the floor with legs crossed or toward the edge of a dining or desk chair. Keep your back relatively straight but not rigid. Close your eyes and allow yourself to breathe normally. Notice the air as it goes in through your nose, travels down to your lungs, and then out again. Pay attention to how your shoulders and chest raise and then lower slightly. Be sensitive to the entire process without altering anything. Stay with your breathing for several minutes, increasing your time as much as you are able.

Warming the Tan T'ien

There are three main energy centers in the body—upper, middle, and lower—all called the tan t'ien. Warming begins in the lower of the three energy centers. This area, fueled by meditation and located an inch and a half below the navel, is the central furnace of the body and is an important center used in martial arts, Eastern medicine, and chi kung as a source for power and energy. With focused attention on this area, energy is gathered and then circulated around the body via certain exercises.

Meditation on Warming Your Lower Tan T'ien

You can locate your tan t'ien by touching your thumbs to your navel. Lay your hands across your abdomen so that your fingers touch, forming an empty triangle between them. Your fingers will be placed over your lower tan t'ien.

Now, place your palms over the tan t'ien; focus all your attention on this area and imagine warmth and energy building. You can use a visualization to help: Imagine that you have a source of comfortable heat located in your abdomen. Feel the warmth beginning in a small area and then spreading outwards. You can use an image of a warm fire or a memory of a hot day in the middle of summer. Suggest to yourself that you feel the warmth building. With practice you will be able to generate the experience of warmth in your tan t'ien. This warm feeling comes from your chi energy.

Extending Your Chi

You can extend your chi using an energy ball. Traditionally, this was imagined as a golden ball, but we often have students imagine a beach ball. Begin with your hands over your tan t'ien until you begin to feel warmth there. Then extend your hands outward, palms facing each other as if you are holding a ball of energy in your hands. You will feel warmth and tingling develop in the palms of your hands as you focus all your attention on the energy ball. Let your energy ball begin to move by shifting your hands around so that one hand holds from above and the other hand holds from below. With practice it will begin to seem as if the energy ball is floating, making your hands move.

Small Circulation Meditation

Most forms of chi kung consider this exercise to be an important skill. Once you have been able to experience some warming or tingling in your tan t'ien, you can learn how to circulate your energy around your body. Visualize the energy moving up from your tan t'ien along a pathway up the middle of your body. Visualize each acupoint (see Lesson Six) and focus your energy about an inch deep. Pay attention to the area until tingling or warmth develops. Another method is to imagine a small ball of energy, about the size of a golf ball, rolling around at the point. Move to each point in sequence, concentrating on each for a minute or two. You may only do one or two points at first. Don't rush

Conception Vessel

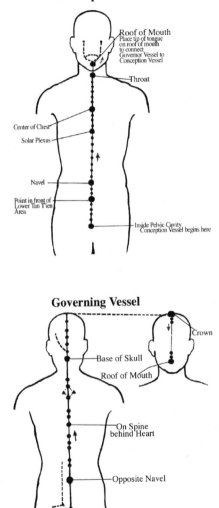

Roof of Mouth
Place tip of tongue on roof of mouth to connect Governor Vessel to Conception Vessel

Throat

Center of Chest

Solar Plexus

Navel

Point in front of Lower Tan Tien Area

Inside Pelvic Cavity Conception Vessel begins here

Governing Vessel

Crown

Base of Skull

Roof of Mouth

On Spine behind Heart

Opposite Navel

Pelvic Floor
Governing Vessel begins here

Internal branch travels to kidneys

Chi

the process. Proceed only as it feels comfortable. If you have difficulty or discomfort after several sincere attempts, stop the meditation and seek guidance from a chi kung or martial arts teacher.

Integrating Wholeness Contemplation

Chi kung not only allows for the integration of the body, it also brings unity for the whole being as One with the universe, One with Tao. When you do your chi kung exercises, allow yourself to make the connections. Every time you breathe in, you are taking in air and energy from the environment. Each breath out sends your energy out into the world. There is no rigid boundary between you and the world.

Free-Flowing Chi Exercise

Chi kung can be a creative process. Artists draw from the flow of chi when they create art the Taoist way (see Lesson Eight).

People have performed many different traditional patterns of chi kung for centuries. But ultimately, these patterns are merely empty containers to be filled with chi. Just as with Tao, the shape of the container is not what is important. Tao goes everywhere. So you can create your own chi kung patterns to let your chi flow freely.

Find a place where you have some open space. Stand in a relaxed position and meditate on your tan t'ien for several minutes until you feel some warming. Next, allow your chi to circulate, as you have in previous exercises. As it does, let your body move with it, as it wants to. Don't force a move, simply wait for movement to happen. If movement does happen, enjoy the flow. If not, enjoy the stillness.

Healthy Living Through Eastern Medicine

I pause and ponder the direction of flow
And wonder where will my life force go?
—C. Alexander Simpkins

Chi is everywhere in various forms, both within your body and outside in your environment. When you are in harmony with Tao, you function at your best. Chi flows freely and you move through life effortlessly. Eastern medicine is the inner Way to correct problems with chi within your body.

Background of Eastern Medicine

Eastern medicine has a long history, dating back thousands of years, with many great minds contributing to its evolution. Based in Taoist principles, Eastern medicine has its own unique methods that include acupuncture, herbs, massage, and chi kung exercise. Chi is fundamental to all of these treatments.

The earliest text of Eastern medicine is the *Yellow Emperor's Inner*

Classic (The Huang Ti Nei Ching) written around 300 B.C. But parts of the text are thought to be much older, dating back to the time of the Yellow Emperor Huang Ti, around 2700 B.C. The book is divided into two parts: "Simple Questions" concerning general theories of medicine and "Spiritual Axis" describing acupuncture. The book shows that the roots of Eastern medicine came from Taoism (Gascoigne 1997, 11).

Taoist health sects developed in the second century A.D. (see Introduction: Historical Background of Taoism). These groups were led by charismatic healers who promised a better life through healthy, moral living. Members were taught about diet and exercise to promote health along with medical prescriptions for illness.

The guidelines set out in the *Yellow Emperor's Inner Classic* were used and developed in new directions. The theory of the Five Elements was combined with the understandings of yin-yang and chi. Meditation techniques and herbal potions were developed to not only prolong life but also to lead to immortality, and Taoist alchemists pursued immortality using these methods. Although the alchemists may not have succeeded in finding the key to everlasting physical life, many of their practices do promote long and healthy living.

Eastern and Western Medicine Compared

Western medicine takes a material view of disease. Medical students learn about the organs by observing and dissecting cadavers to learn the physical structure of the human body. The Western view takes for granted the belief that illness is the incorrect functioning of the body. Through proper tests, doctors determine the affected structure and offer treatments—drugs that change the chemistry of the diseased organ or system, or surgery that cuts out or corrects the diseased organ.

Eastern doctors take a very different point of view. Instead of emphasizing structure, they think about the interaction of energy systems. They ask, What does this system do and what does it affect? Thus the kidneys aren't simply the two organs in our lower abdomen. They are analyzed in terms of a flow of energy that affects what they do, which includes the lower back, pelvis, reproductive system, and even the knees and the bones. All of these systems function as a unit, and so the Eastern doctor considers disease in terms of the whole person.

Eastern medicine developed the energy approach for directing chi to heal diseases, and there are many examples of successful cures and ever-increasing numbers of research projects confirming these positive results (Kaptchuk 1983, 20).

Eastern doctors use many of the same terms for the parts of the body, such as Kidney, Spleen, Heart, and Liver, but in each case the term refers to the functional energy system rather than the specific organ. (Eastern medical books capitalize these words to distinguish them from the Western use.)

The Five Elements and Yin-Yang

Eastern medicine draws from the Taoist orientation to the world, incorporating the Five Elements and Yin-Yang into the understanding of the human body. Since the human body is part of the universe and the universe is made up of wood, fire, earth, metal, and water, so, too, these elements act physiologically within the human body. Each element is related to an organ: water is related to the Kidney/Bladder, wood to Liver/Gall Bladder, fire to Heart/Small Intestine, earth to Spleen/Stomach, and metal to Lung/Large Intestine. Similar to how the elements enhance and restrain each other, so the organ systems of the body stimulate and inhibit each other.

Each organ system is categorized as yin or yang (see the chart on page 69). Furthermore, the *positioning* of the organs is in terms of yin and yang, whether they are interior (yin) or exterior (yang), in front (yin) or back (yang), lower (yin) or upper (yang). Thus, the use of yin and yang in the human body is not simplistic. For example, the heart, located in the upper part of the body, is in a yang location, yet it is categorized as a yin organ. So, yin-yang is a subtle system that attempts to realistically help describe the complexities of the human body.

Meridians

Chi flows through twelve main channels running throughout the body, called meridians, or *jung-luo*. Jung-luo translates as a connecting thread in a fabric, and this is how the meridians function. The meridians are a network that links together all the substances and organs, the inner with the outer, by circulating chi and blood. A continuous and smooth flow through the meridians is essential for health.

Meridians are not visible like blood vessels or arteries. Think of them more like energy streams. When there is an excess of chi, the energy stream will swell. During dry periods, the stream will shrink. Sometimes an obstruction causes the stream to change course. Chi energy gathers at points called cavities, which can divert the flow of chi. So chi can be influenced by placing acupuncture needles into these cavities. Massaging the cavities can also affect chi's movement. The flow of chi will increase or decrease to help stimulate all the different functions of the body (e.g., improve digestion, enhance energy).

While meridians cannot be literally touched or seen, researchers in China, Russia, and Europe have found some empirical evidence that they do exist. Using a highly sensitive potentiometer, researchers observed constant resistance along the meridians but fluctuating resistance everywhere else (Palos 1972, 77). There is a stable system along the path of the meridians.

Each meridian has a name and tends to govern certain functions. The twelve meridians are Lung, Large Intestine, Stomach, Spleen, Heart, Small Intestine, Bladder, Kidney, Pericardium, Triple Warmer, Gall Bladder, and Liver (see figures on pages 70–72). These meridian pathways are paired with organs that are either yin or yang. Yin organs are involved with the fundamental substances in the body while yang organs tend to control the taking in of food, its absorption, and elimination.

Fu/Yin Organs	Zang/Yang Organs
Heart	Small Intestine
Lungs	Large Intestine
Spleen	Stomach
Liver	Gall Bladder
Kidneys	Bladder
Pericardium	Triple Warmer

There are eight special meridians. Two of them—the Governing Vessel and the Conception Vessel (see diagrams in Lesson Five)—are used extensively in chi kung. There are also lesser meridians, like tributaries and brooks that interconnect the larger ones and share points along the way.

Eastern medicine includes two systems that do not correspond to any organ at all: the Triple Warmer and Pericardium. The Triple Warmer is not an actual organ, and the Chinese texts are somewhat vague about its structure (Kaptchuk 1983, 68). It refers to fire and heat and controls water. Just as water controls fire in the natural world, we can recognize the usefulness of the Triple Warmer for regulating how water is moved through the body. Since the human body is primarily water, this system is extremely important for healthy functioning. The Pericardium helps to regulate the heart. Although it is not an organ of its own, it serves a vital purpose in regulating the whole body.

Eastern healers believe the energy systems are stable and consistent and include characteristics that make them accessible to observation even though they are not physical structures. When surges or blockages in the energy streams happen, doctors can take the necessary actions to bring the system back into balance by restoring the correct energy flow of chi (see Lesson Five for more details on chi).

Lung Meridian

Large Intestine Meridian

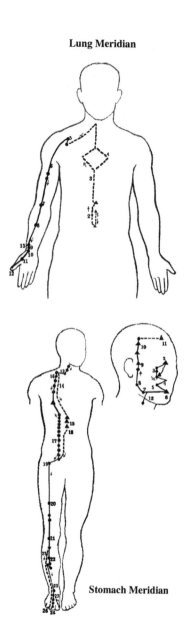

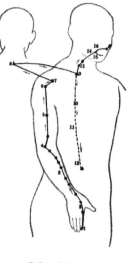

Spleen Meridian

Stomach Meridian

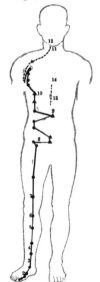

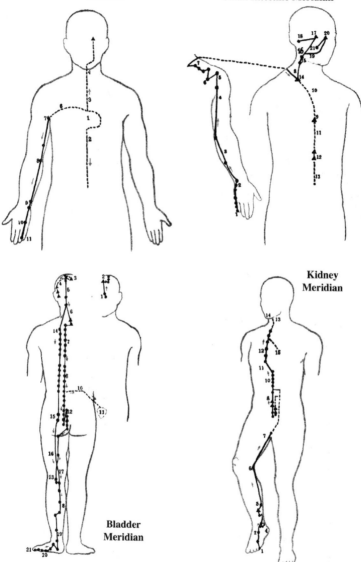

Heart Meridian

Small Intestine Meridian

Kidney Meridian

Bladder Meridian

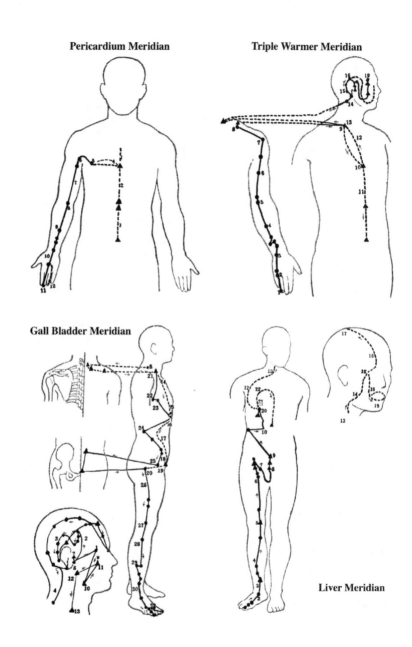

Pericardium Meridian

Triple Warmer Meridian

Gall Bladder Meridian

Liver Meridian

Tao in Ten

Meridian Exercises to Prevent Blockages

Do-in is a form of exercise people can do themselves to improve health, enhance vitality, and increase spiritual awareness. Drawn from the Taoist method Tao Yin, the gentle approach to the Way, these exercises are specifically designed to unblock chi in the meridians.

To perform these exercises, hold each position, at the farthest comfortable point for you, for two slow breaths.

Lung and Large Intestine Meridians Exercise (Figure 18)

Stand with your feet shoulder-width apart. Lock your fingers together behind your back, palms facing out. Lift your head and drop your chin back. Then raise your arms up as you bend forward from the waist and hold. Switch the interlocking of your fingers, so the other thumb is on top, to unblock both sides of the meridians. Greater tightness in one finger position over the other tells you that one side is more blocked.

Spleen-Pancreas and Stomach Meridians Exercise (Figure 19)

Kneel on the floor and sit down over your feet with your right big toe crossed over your left. Holding your arms overhead with fingers interlocking, gently arch your back and hold.

Heart and Small Intestine Meridians Exercise (Figure 20)

Sit with knees bent outward and the soles of your feet pressing against each other. Hold your feet together with your hands around the toes. Slowly bend forward from the waist until your forehead approaches your thumbs.

Liver and Gall Bladder Meridians Exercise (Figure 21)

Sit on the floor with legs extended as wide apart as is comfortable. Hold your hands over your left knee and then slide your hands slowly toward your left foot as you bend forward. When your hands reach your foot, hold on and let your forehead drop toward your knee—touching if possible. If you do not have the flexibility to go this far

Figure 18 · Lung and Large Intestine Meridians Exercise

Figure 19 · Spleen-Pancreas and Stomach Meridians Exercise

Figure 20 · Heart and Small Intestine Meridians Exercise

Figure 21 · Liver and Gall Bladder Meridians Exercise

Figure 22 · Kidney and Bladder Meridians Exercise

Figure 23 · Pericardium and Triple Warmer Meridians Exercise

down, stretch as far as you comfortably can and hold. Repeat on the right side.

Kidney and Bladder Meridians Exercise (Figure 22)
Sit on the floor with your legs extended straight in front of you. Slide your hands down to grasp your feet as your head touches your knees and hold.

Pericardium and Triple Warmer Meridians Exercise (Figure 23)
Sit in a lotus position if you can. Otherwise use a half-lotus or cross-legged position. Place your right hand on your left knee and your left hand on your right knee. Press each knee down as you slowly bend forward toward the floor and hold.

Diagnosis

The Eastern doctor looks at the unity of the whole person when making a diagnosis. The healthy person lives in harmonious interactive unity, One with Tao. Illness, then, is a disruption of the normal harmony and proper flow of energy in the body. Any problem in one area ripples through the entire body and will show up throughout the body energy system. Since all is interrelated, dysfunction leads to consistent signs.

This holistic perspective leads to different diagnostic criteria from that used in the West, where problems are often categorized as the type of illness. An example might help to make the distinction clear. All people diagnosed by Western doctors with chronic hypertension do not necessarily have the same condition to Eastern practitioners. Eastern healers look at a variety of factors and try to discern patterns that make sense within yin-yang and Five Elements theory. For example, a person might have a Liver-Fire condition with symptoms of headache, dizziness, red eyes and face, and irritability. Another person diagnosed with hypertension by Western medicine could suffer from a condition Eastern medicine would consider to be

Liver Yang Increasing. This individual might have symptoms of dizziness along with ringing in the ears, blurred vision, and insomnia. Both people may present with hypertension, but each case would be treated differently to resolve the underlying condition that is leading to the hypertension.

Eastern medicine practitioners are trained to diagnose by observing, listening, touching, and questioning the patient. Observations are gathered and considered to perceive the consistent pattern of disharmony.

Diagnosis takes place through the trained senses of the doctor. Observing the patient includes observing the patient's appearance, behavior, emotional responsiveness, posture, vitality, facial color, and coating of the tongue. For example, a depleted, weak-looking, pale appearance accompanied by fatigue, lack of vitality, and sagging posture tend to indicate depletion, an imbalance toward yin and lowered chi.

The tongue is inspected for its signs of underlying conditions. A normal tongue is flexible and healthy pink in color, filling the mouth without being too large or too small, smooth with a whitish coating. Unusual variations are noted for their possible indications of patterns. A doctor skilled in Eastern medicine is best qualified to diagnose from the tongue.

Doctors use their sense of touch to diagnose the pulse. Pulse can be affected by gender, age, season, time of day, and illness. Conditions are expressed in changes in the pulse from what is normal for that person. In the West, we count the beats of the heart, measured as pulse rate, note the blood pressure, and listen for general strength or weakness of the pulse. The Eastern practitioner, however, goes much further in evaluation. Doctors feel the patient's pulse at the wrist using the tips of their index, middle, and ring fingers. Sensitive pressure is applied in three ways: light, medium, and deep. The speed, forcefulness, rhythm, and other subtle qualities of the pulse help determine diagnosis.

The pulse might be characterized as weak or strong, pounding or slippery. Each of more than twenty-eight, often poetic, qualities is linked to the underlying condition. For example, a strong, pounding pulse often coupled with warm arms indicates a yang imbalance.

Treatment

Each person's condition is a unique interplay between yin and yang. The goal of treatment is to bring a healthy balance, restoring dynamic equilibrium.

Various methods may be chosen by the skilled practitioner to address the patient's individual needs. Treatment can be direct or indirect. Doctors treat the condition, not just the symptom, so treatment may sometimes seem unrelated, such as massaging the hand for a headache.

Symptoms—wet, dry, hot, cold—are a clue to the condition. For example, a fire condition will give symptoms of heat expressed as elevated temperature, flushed skin, achy body, and harsh voice tones. Heat condition is yang, so active, emotionally volatile reactions might be expected. The pattern of symptoms is indicative of the underlying condition.

Treatment procedures seek the associated organ system disharmony. The practitioner restores balance with the appropriate combination of acupuncture, meditation, massage, exercise, and herbs.

Using Acupuncture for Treatment

Acupuncture is a treatment method that utilizes the meridian theory to bring about cures. The doctor stimulates and restrains appropriate points on the meridians related to the disharmony.

This ancient therapy has been practiced in China for thousands of year and was described in the ancient text *The Yellow Emperor's Classic of Internal Medicine.*

The word *acupuncture* comes from the Latin words *acus,* meaning needle, and *pungere,* meaning to puncture. The acupuncturist places extremely thin needles into the acupoints along the meridians. Correct placement of the needles increases, decreases, or redirects the flow of chi as needed to restore balance.

Each meridian has a pathway that extends around the body, so treatments that may seem unrelated from a Western perspective are logically linked from the Eastern point of view. For example, the doctor might place a needle into a point on the hand in order to treat heart disease because the Heart meridian and the Pericardium meridian both extend down the arm. The connection might not be surprising when we consider that people who suffer a heart attack often feel pain radiating down their arm. Often, distant points in hands or feet help central organ systems recover harmony.

After the diagnosis has been made, the patient lies on a flat, slightly padded table in a quiet room. Needles are inserted at key points for meridians that have been diagnosed as being blocked, stagnant, or overly stimulated. The needles are so thin, the diameter of a hair, that usually patients barely feel them. What they are more likely to experience is the stimulation and enhanced movement of chi.

The manner in which the treatment needles are inserted determines how chi is affected. Needles may be pushed in straight or at an angle. They can also be twirled in, rotating for greater stimulation. Sometimes they are given small currents of electricity or heat. Needles can tonify, stimulating chi that is stagnant or sluggish, or they can relax, smoothing out or pacifying chi that is overactive.

Insertion of needles might be on the meridian of the affected area or on the opposite meridian of the yin-yang pair. Sometimes the doctor will stimulate a yin point and a yang point at the same time. General strengthening is also done to stimulate points that are associated with a particular condition. In this way the patient gains the vitality needed to combat the illness.

The needles are left in place by the practitioner for fifteen to twenty minutes, although the amount of time can be as long as several hours depending on the problem and the particular patient. During this period the patient rests quietly. Some people feel tingling, warmth, relaxation, or other sensations related to chi as energy shifts and flows from the effects of the needles. The sensations from a needle placed in the foot might be felt locally or elsewhere along the meridian—even as far away as the top of the head! The doctor may return to twirl a needle or two during the rest period to facilitate chi circulation.

Finally, all the needles are removed. Sometimes the doctor will prescribe herbs, massage, or chi kung to augment healing between treatments. Most people feel calm and relaxed when they leave their acupuncture session.

Acupressure

Professional acupressure practitioners treat many of the same ailments as acupuncturists. One of the advantages of acupressure is that it is mild, noninvasive, and easy to do, so you can assist in your treatment at home of many common complaints. For example, on your own, you can deal with such minor conditions as headaches, sinus problems, and pain in the lower back and upper back, arms, and hands. Acupressure is not a substitute for medical treatment, but it can encourage healing and help in many situations

Types of Acupressure Various systems of acupressure exist, but the main intention is to diagnose and treat problems in chi flow: too much chi means the chi flow has to be reduced; too little chi means the chi flow has to be increased until balance is reached.

There are also ways to increase or decrease chi that correspond with the Five Element theory, with the acupressure point that is associated with the elements. So, for example, patients who are suffering from heat could increase their comfort by massaging the water points, which are cooling and thus will neutralize the imbalance.

There are a number of simple ways that you can use this approach. For more serious conditions, seek guidance from a professional. Often the Eastern healer will encourage self-treatment to maintain progress. Think of yourself as a unit, not just an ailing part. Treat the whole.

Massaging the Points Acupressure massage technique involves pressing on the acupoint using the index finger. The amount of pressure used to massage is less than five pounds—a small amount. Press for thirty seconds to a minute on each point.

A second method is to massage in a small circular motion with light pressure on the acupoint using the thumb or forefinger. Massage for thirty seconds to a minute.

Do not press so hard as to cause pain when using either of these techniques. Pay careful attention to what you are doing.

Sample Treatments The logic of treatment is similar to acupuncture and uses the meridian charts to help direct where you should massage. Specific points have typically been found to help with certain conditions.

Nasal congestion caused by allergies or the common cold may be a problem that people can treat at home by massaging certain acupoints usually related to the symptom. One point that can help this condition is located on the Governing Vessel, located between the eyebrows. Another place to massage is two parallel points, on the Large Intestine meridian at both sides of the nostrils. Massaging points on the hand can also help reduce nasal congestion. A point known as the Meeting Valley, located on the fork between the thumb and the index finger on top of the hand, may also help. Lightly massaging all these points begins a process that enhances the flow of chi and increases the immune response. In addition, massage the neck muscles where they attach at the base of the skull. Remember, if it hurts, lighten up on the pressure or do not massage or press the point at all. In this situation, pain is a signal to pay attention, not something to ignore.

Hand pain is a common problem faced by office workers as well as manual laborers. Massage the point located behind the thumb where the thumb meets the wrist along the Large Intestine meridian to help reduce pain and encourage chi flow to the thumb area. A point on the Lung meridian, two inches beyond the hand at the base of the thumb and the back of the wrist, can also be massaged to help with thumb pain. The index finger has massage points at the base of the hand on the palm side at the juncture with the wrist. One at the side of the wrist is located on the Pericardium meridian; the other is on the Heart meridian, directly in the center of the wrist. Massaging these areas gently may help soothe minor pains in the hand.

Acupoint Awareness You can enhance your treatment by becoming aware of the acupuncture/acupressure points. Pick a point from one of the charts that you are using in a treatment. Begin by massaging the area lightly for thirty seconds or so. Feel the sensations as you massage and after you stop. You might feel a sensation running along the whole meridian or at some point along the meridian. With practice you can become aware of points and meridians by noticing any subtle sensations that might normally go unnoticed. If you don't feel anything at first, keep your mind open to the possibility and continue to experiment. You may not feel improvement immediately, but it may still help. Use your meditative attention on points whenever you do a treatment. Remember, where mind goes, chi flows.

Tapping Massage to Relax and Energize
A broad range of acupressure points can be stimulated this way. Close your eyes. Using one hand, tap the opposite shoulder with your fingertips. Keep your fingers loose as you tap steadily and lightly, using only ounces of force. Cover the shoulder and neck areas that you can reach for about thirty seconds. Then stop and feel the sensations. You might notice a slight tingling, warmth, or comfortable relaxing. This is the chi flowing into the area. You can use this technique to relax your arms and legs as well.

1. *At lower edge of jaw, below ear (both sides)* Massage circularly and then press lightly and steadily. For temporary help with lower tooth or jaw discomfort.

2. *At cheekbone point (both sides)* Massage and press. For temporary help with upper tooth and jaw discomfort.

3. *One inch above eyebrows (both sides)* Massage and press. Dental and sinus discomfort.

4. *Between eyebrows at bridge of nose (both sides)* Squeeze between thumb and forefinger. Sinus congestion of colds or to stop a mild sneeze.

5. *At nostrils both sides of nose* Press lightly. Nasal congestion.

6. *Shoulder point* Massage and press. Shoulder, elbow, and arm pain.

7. *Below collarbone between second and third ribs* Massage and press. To help reduce coughing.

8. *Three inches below navel* Use circular motions, lightly; massage the area, then light pressure. Abdominal discomfort.

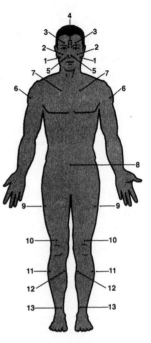

Figure 24

9. *Midlevel at outside of thigh (When standing, drop arms to your side. Point is at the level of your middle finger.* Massage then press. Tension in legs, hips, and knees.

10. *Two inches above kneecap* Massage and press. Abdominal and menstrual discomfort.

11. *Outside of calf about four inches below knee* Massage and press. Lower leg, knee, ankle, and foot pains and strains. Encourages strengthening of these areas. Helps allergies.

12. *Inside of calf* Massage and press. Lower leg, knee, ankle, and foot pains and strains. Encourages strengthening of these areas. Lower back discomfort.

13. *Three inches above ankle* Stroke linearly. Menstrual discomfort and cramps.

1. *Below skull, top of both muscles of neck at the base of the skull* Massage and press. Tension headaches and sinus congestion.

2. *On trapezius, where shoulders and neck meet* Squeeze between thumb and fingers, then massage. Tight shoulders, overall tension, and tension headaches.

3. *Behind scapula* Stroke vertically between two sets of points. Upper back and shoulder strain.

4. *Along two muscle strands* Stroke vertically between two sets of points. Upper middle back strain.

5. *Below elbow at hollow point* between muscles Massage and press. Wrist and arm discomfort, enhance immune system.

6. *Below fourth and fifth ribs, on muscle band* Massage then press. Helps with congestion and tight upper back, shoulders, and arms.

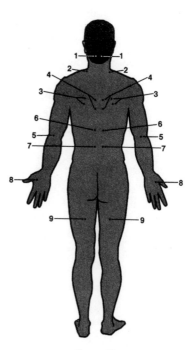

Figure 25

7. *Lower back at second lumbar vertebrae, base of both muscles* Massage toward waist. For tight back if not injured.

8. *Top of muscle on fork between thumb and index finger* Massage and press as in #1. Helps with nasal congestion, colds, headaches, and dental discomfort.

9. *Center of leg biceps* Massage then press. Tight muscles and menstrual discomfort.

Tui Na

Tui na is another form of massage used in Eastern healing. Rather than pressing and moving the fingers around as you do in acupressure, in tui na you use other techniques, such as gently holding the cord of a muscle between your fingers and rolling it, somewhat like working with clay. Another technique is to stroke briskly, using the back of the hand. You can also do tapping with the fingertips or the outside edge of your hand using very light pressure, less than a pound. The taps stimulate the muscles and relax the larger area, affecting the associated organ energy system.

These massage techniques are very effective with muscle cramps and weak muscles. Slow massage can help you relax. When done quickly, the massage can help to stimulate. The tui na approach enhances the flow of chi through the meridians. You can use it in association with Western medical treatment to enhance your comfort as it blends with many forms of treatment. Improved chi flow, as well as enhanced comfort and relaxation may help your immune system, important for health and recovery.

Sample Treatments Combined with herbs and therapeutic exercises, many minor problems may improve quickly with tui na.

A headache with no medical problem associated to it—for example, from tiredness or muscle tension—can be helped by stroking the neck and shoulder muscles at the back of the neck. You can also use a circular motion of the fingertips around the temple. Spreading pressure with the fingertips from the center of the forehead outward to the ears, systematically for ten minutes or so, without too much pressure, may help release some of the tensions associated with the headache. The hand can also be massaged around the wrist in circular motion.

To relieve menstrual cramps and muscle tightness in the legs, massage the ankles by stroking upward the inside and outside of the anklebone with the thumbs. Any way that you can encourage the flow of chi is helpful and is a natural use of the Taoist healing methods.

Herbs

Herbal treatment coordinates well with acupressure, acupuncture, and massage. It can help to balance and encourage the yin and the yang in your body and your relationship with your environment. There are herbs that cool and herbs that warm; some herbs have a drying effect while others bring moisture, some encourage decongestion and circulation. Herbs may also help chi flow.

When a preparation is prescribed it is usually a combination of several herbs specifically chosen for the person to help them with a particular condition. Research presently being conducted around the world is exploring these treatments and their efficacy and is continuing to find that many of them are effective or compatible.

As the popularity of alternative medicine increases in the West, specific, high-quality herbs are becoming easier to buy. Many health food stores and even grocery stores now carry herbal remedies for common problems. These can be helpful when you are in the midst of discomfort. But keep in mind that these premixed remedies may not address your unique problem, which a trained professional will take into account.

Restoring Balance Through Herbs You can maintain your health with supplements that enhance the flow of chi. Some herbs stimulate the body while others relax it. If you feel yourself beginning to get off balance, or simply want to maintain a positive trend in your energy, an herbal tea might help. Balance yin with yang and yang with yin to maintain a healthy harmony.

Ginseng is generally prescribed as a tonifying herb to improve immune system function and encourage chi. The tendency of chi is to enhance warmth and vitality. Ginseng can assist when you are feeling depleted, fatigued, and stressed (Veninga 1973).

Peppermint is an example of an herb that helps to cool the system, increase circulation, and thus bring relief to conditions with opposite qualities. Another commonly available herb, licorice, has cooling properties as well. Licorice also enhances immune response. Herbs are often used in combination to facilitate or moderate effects.

Finding an Eastern Medicine Practitioner

Sometimes home treatment can only be a supplement to care from a qualified practitioner. And fortunately, Eastern medicine doctors are now practicing throughout the world. It is even possible to obtain training in Eastern medicine in the West as well as the East. Candidates undergo an extensive program of study that can result in a master's of Oriental medicine or a doctor of Oriental medicine degree. They must have an internship experience and pass a licensing examination before they are ready to practice. You can locate a practitioner by consulting your telephone book or a nearby, accredited college of Oriental medicine. Also, some Western doctors work with Eastern doctors in what is now called integrative medicine. Eastern and Western treatments can be complimentary.

Prevention

Awareness along with massage, herbs, and exercise can be used to prevent chi imbalances. By enhancing the body's immune system, you can strengthen and prevent problems from starting. Long ago in China, the doctor was paid when people were healthy. When their patients became sick, payment was withheld. The idea was that just as you should not begin to dig a well for water after you are thirsty, it is too late to treat disease when people are sick. Of course, Eastern doctors did have to treat illness, but they tried their best to prevent it. Keeping your energy in balance tends to bring about an overall experience of well-being, improved concentration, and greater vitality.

Healthy Eating

Eastern medicine looks at the whole person, and eating is considered an important aspect of keeping healthy. Foods have different qualities, so healthy eating involves a balance of these different qualities. We should be concerned with the correct balance of what we eat. Moderation is central.

Foods are classified as yin, yang, or neutral, and Eastern medicine believes you can maintain your health by eating a balance of yin and yang foods. When people are ill, an Eastern healer might prescribe a greater quantity of one type of food more than another to restore balance, helping the treatment regimen to be more effective.

The categories correspond to what you would expect: Yin foods are cold, such as cucumbers and watermelon, and cool, such as bananas and apples. Eating these foods tends to remove heat. Yang foods are hot, such as peppers and onions, and warm, such as peaches and cherries. Yang foods can help to warm you and dispel excess yin. Neutral foods, such as lemons and strawberries, do not influence heat or cold. These effects synergize with herbs, acupressure, and acupuncture.

Foods are also classified by flavor: sour, bitter, salty, sweet, and bland. Each can have certain functions. For example, spicy foods, as you might expect, help to promote chi circulation. Bitter foods can remove excessive heat. These qualities can be used to help you stay in balance.

Much of the dietary advice given by Eastern healers for prevention appeals to common sense.

Martial Arts

Developing Inner Strength and Using It Well

Renounce outer force
and be at ease with the world.
Cultivate inner strength
and trust the enduring center
Expect a long life
and die fulfilled.
—*Tao Te Ching* 33, Grigg 1995, 103

Being a strong person is highly valued and useful in coping with the difficulties of life. People sometimes think that being powerful will help. Taoists take the opposite position: The weak overcomes the strong, the soft outlasts the hard. People can accomplish difficult tasks in life by relaxing and becoming flexible. Coping with force without using force is surprisingly effective and very natural when you learn how to do it correctly. Chi circulates freely, producing great power and capacity to deal with life.

Many people think martial arts is just about self-defense and fighting, but longtime practitioners of these arts know that these are limited perceptions. Ultimately, the martial arts are a journey of inner development. By learning how to handle force coming toward him, the martial artist not only learns about defense, he also learns how to face life's challenges with inner strength. The martial artist develops a calm center in harmony with the forces around him. Masters of the martial arts can handle any attack without losing their center. And this generalizes to all of life. Whenever difficult challenges come along, the skilled martial artist has the inner strength to cope well.

The Power of Chi

Martial artists build internal power by developing their chi. Practitioners learn to harness the power of chi to perform amazing feats of strength—they can break stacks of wood or subdue a larger opponent seemingly without effort. But this power does not come from big muscles. Although some martial artists build muscular strength, the true source of their power comes from the internal development of chi.

We conducted an empirical experiment to further our understanding of the power of chi in the martial artist (Simpkins 1992, 36–52). We devised the experiment to measure the speed and force of punches performed by two groups of people: accomplished martial artists and physically fit, athletic non–martial artists. In theory, these two groups of physically fit adults should have the same speed and power as others in their weight class. What we found was that martial artists had statistically greater power and faster speeds than non–martial artists. We hypothesized that the difference came from chi: The martial artists had developed their chi whereas the non–martial artists had not. Interestingly, women were just as capable as men of the same body weight. Chi makes no gender distinctions!

Chi is traditionally referred to as inner force. The martial artists in this study certainly seemed to manifest it. There was a dynamic, almost electric quality to the energy expressed during the experiment. Participants found themselves deeply focused in mind, body, and spirit.

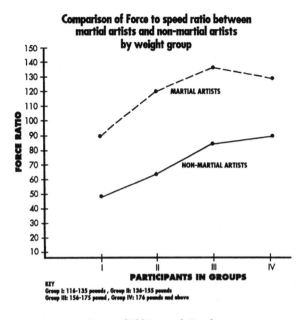

Comparison of Force to speed ratio between martial artists and non-martial artists by weight group

MARTIAL ARTISTS

NON-MARTIAL ARTISTS

FORCE RATIO

PARTICIPANTS IN GROUPS

KEY
Group I: 116-135 pounds , Group II: 136-155 pounds
Group III: 156-175 pound , Group IV: 176 pounds and above

Power of Chi Research Results

Internal Martial Arts

Traditionally, there were three internal Chinese martial arts that based their source of power on developing chi: hsing-i, pa kua, and tai chi. All three draw from the philosophical roots of Taoism, but each has a slightly different emphasis, incorporating some Taoist principles more than others.

In the past, hsing-i was taught first, pa kua second, and tai chi last, because the three arts progressively developed from the outer to the inner, from hard to soft, maturing the spirit, evolving the mind, and developing chi.

All three internal arts emphasize sensitivity and flexibility to activate chi. The secret to true power resides in softness and relaxation. Students achieve softness by learning to be relaxed in their muscles.

They perform movements slowly and evenly, prolonging each posture. An inner feel for balance and relaxed, harmonious movement develops.

Breathing must also become soft so that it harmonizes with action. In many soft techniques, the practitioner breathes in as the arms move one way, then out as they move in the other. The ultimate goal is for the breathing to become natural, like a child's. In the *Tao Te Ching*, Lao-tzu asked, By meditating on breathing until you become soft, can you be like an infant?

Hsing-I (The Form of Mind)

Hsing-i is a linear art, where the practitioner moves forward, meeting force with force. "Hsing" means form and "i" means intention or will, showing how the development of a strong spirit is primary (Wildish 2000, 132). But as an inner art, hsing-i develops the inner mind first and the body strength follows.

The core of hsing-i is five basic patterns. These five sets of movements integrate with the Five Elements and the process where one element generates another (see Lesson Four). So, for example, the martial art movement called pounding corresponds with the element fire, the organ heart, and the chi action of sudden release, like an arrow shot into the air.

Name	Element	Organ	Action of Chi
Splitting	Metal	Lung	Rises and falls like chopping with an ax
Crushing	Wood	Liver	Expands and contracts simultaneously
Drilling	Water	Kidney	Flows in curving eddies or shoots like lightning
Pounding	Fire	Heart	Fires suddenly like a projectile
Crossing	Earth	Spleen	Strikes forward with rounded energy

Hsing-i draws from the Taoist philosophy of yin and yang by incorporating yin-yang pairs: stillness and movement, contraction and expansion, and backward and forward. The practitioner learns to be in balance, centered. Chi flows through the body, giving inner strength to the movements. But unlike tai chi, motions are both hard and soft, both sides of the yin-yang.

Hsing-i uses the movements of animals, not to imitate their actions but to draw from the will or intention of the animal. Since developing a strong will is central in hsing-i, practitioners draw inspiration for their forceful movements from the spontaneous will of each animal.

At first, will-training is deliberate. But through focused attention, students train their minds until they no longer have to focus attention. "Therefore boxing and Tao are the same. In an emergency you do not try to hear or see: you merely avoid automatically" (Smith 1974, 112).

Hsing-I Exercise: Pounding (Adapted from Basic Form Four)
(Figures 26–28)
According to classic hsing-i tradition, this exercise can calm the mind. Step forward with your right foot as you raise your left arm overhead, bent at the elbow, fist tight for an upward block. At the same time, extend your right arm lower than the left, into a middle-level punch. Then step forward with your left foot and repeat the pattern on the other side. Keep your mind focused on moving forward despite all odds.

Pa Kua (The Eight Diagrams)

Pa kua is based on the concept of circular change. Drawn from the trigrams in the *I-Ching*, practitioners synchronize with the movement of the universe through its circular cycles from yin to yang and back to yin continuously. By accepting the cycle of change as its primary principle, the student of pa kua is ready for everything. "Change is its strength and its totality" (Smith 1977, 14).

Figure 26   Figure 27

Figure 28

Hsing-I Exercise: Pounding (Adapted from Basic Form Four)

Considered flexible and powerful, the palm is the basic weapon used in this style. Each of the eight trigrams corresponds to a position of the palm, and as the trigrams shift from completely yang (three solid lines) to completely yin (three broken lines) the palm gradually turns from palm up to palm down and then back to up again.

The single palm change is one of the fundamental actions in this art. The palm change takes your palm from one position to another as you move along a circle. The purpose of a palm change is to permit a rapid change in direction without losing touch with your opponent. Movement is always whole-body movement, and a palm change is integrated into this action. Many methods of palm changes make up a complex array of strikes and grabs performed in this style.

Palm Awareness Try analyzing your movements in terms of where your palms are facing. You can apply this even to closed fist techniques, considering which direction the palm of your fist faces. You might be surprised how descriptive and helpful it is to think about where your palm is, how it changes position and direction as it moves, and what possibilities are created as a result.

Mental Attitude Like the other internal arts, a calm mind is your starting point. "To stand still results in the mind's settlement, mind's settlement in tranquility . . ." (Smith 1977, 114). A still mind, a relaxed body, and slow movements allow for the development of the sensitivity needed to sense and feel the opponent's force. How the student does physically is only a result of what he or she does mentally. Mind directs, strength follows, and chi flows.

As the mind focuses on the "feel" of movement, the practitioner develops an intensified experience of self. Paradoxically, the effect of intensified self-awareness leads to a forgetting of the ego that merges the individual with the universal, One with Tao.

Breathing, like the other internal arts, begins with the stored energy in the lower tan t'ien and moves through the entire body to cir-

Figure 29

Figure 30

Figure 31

Whole Body Palm Flow Warm-Up

Tao in Ten

Figure 32

Figure 33

Figure 34

Walking the Circle Exercise

culate chi. Movements are harmonized with breathing that is natural and soft. Use the meditation exercises from Lesson Five to approach the movement exercises that follow.

Whole Body Palm Flow Warm-Up (Figures 29–31)
Stand with your legs two shoulder-widths apart and knees bent in a horse stance. Bring your left hand down to your side, palm facing to the right and bring your arm around in front as if scooping water that is about knee level. Bring your palm around over your head, as if you drop the water on your head and circle around to begin again. As you perform this exercise, move slowly, gently breathe in as you come across below and out as you come across above. Try to coordinate your whole body together as you circle around. Let your chi circulate through your whole body as you flow through the motions. When you feel ready, switch to the other side.

Walking the Circle Exercise (Figures 32–34)
The fundamental principle of circular change is expressed in a set of practices known as "Walking the Circle." Walking the Circle footwork follows a circular pattern. The circle teaches the student to follow, evade, and change direction, always along a circular path.

Imagine a circle on the floor, six feet in diameter. Place your feet on the edge of this imaginary circle. Begin with both feet on the circle, toes facing forward, knees bent slightly, right hand extended out toward the center of the circle with your palm also facing the center and left hand drawn in across your body, palm down. With your right hand extended, walk in a clockwise direction. Bring the back foot up very slowly, pause slightly and balance and then place the foot down ahead, gently, heel first. Walk around the circle, stepping with one foot and then the other in this slow, relaxed manner as your hands remain in position. Perform the motions smoothly with your whole body flowing together. After walking for a period of time, pivot to the right as you shift your hands, so that the left hand comes around to face the inside of the circle, palm toward the center, while the right hand shifts downward across your body, palm down. Then continue walking the circle in a counterclockwise direction. Breathe with each movement, relax, and make all motions slow and continuous.

Pa kua has many more circle-walking techniques that offer effective methods for self-defense and self-development. If you enjoyed this exercise you may want to seek a recognized pa kua instructor who can guide you more deeply into the art.

Tai Chi (The Great Ultimate)

A quiet breeze gently circles around the group as they move in unison, slowly, calmly together in harmony with their gentle movements. Each person is centered, attention turned inward. Rounded movements are graceful like the rustling of the leaves or the bending of tall grass in the wind. These students are practicing the internal martial art of tai chi.

Tai chi is the most commonly known form of soft-style arts. This art is called the Grand Ultimate because it is considered the highest form of internal training. Tai chi begins in Taoist philosophy and remains true to the principles. The manual *Tai Chi Classic* by the founder of tai chi, Chang San-feng, opens with this statement: "Tai Chi is evolved from Wu Chi. It is the spring of activity and inactivity and the mother of yin and yang" (Lee 1968, 34)

Tai chi practitioners do not use muscle strength. According to the *Tai Chi Classic*, "It is only from the greatest pliability and from yielding completely that you can attain power and ascendancy" (Liang 1977, 4).

The fundamental principle is to concentrate chi in the lower tan t'ien. Using chi kung breathing meditation, practitioners learn how to sink their energy into their tan t'ien. Through slow, rounded, relaxed movements, chi begins to circulate throughout the body.

The principles of yin and yang give form to the practice. "Yin and Yang must complement each other; to understand this is to understand force" (Lee 1968, 41). Based in yin and yang, tai chi has two opposite methods: moving away and sticking. Moving away means to yield in the same direction as the opponent's force, thereby neutralizing the attack. Sticking is the opposite. When the opponent retreats, the practitioner sticks, moving back with the force. This has the same neutralizing effect on the opponent's force.

But the point of tai chi is not simply overcoming opponents. There is a higher purpose:

> A gradual understanding of force would come from familiarity with the techniques and, from understanding of force, would come spiritual illumination. (Lee 1968, 36)

The way to discover this spiritual awakening comes from practice of the sequence of postures. People perform them over and over, learning to let go of tightness or sharp motions.

Movements are also done with a partner, called Pushing Hands or Sticking Hands in hsing-i. All of these exercises teach how to follow and redirect without apparent opposition. You lose aggression and tension as you gain calm and inner strength. From a small loss may come a small gain, but from a great loss comes great gain.

When practitioners become skilled at Pushing Hands, they can sense the slightest opposing force and can respond immediately. The *Tai Chi Classic* states that this sensitivity is so acute that even a feather can't be added, nor can a fly alight without the practitioner feeling it (Lee 1968, 39).

Thus the practice of tai chi is an expression of Taoism. Try the exercises to feel Taoism in motion.

Tai Chi Exercises

Before you begin, focus your attention on your tan t'ien to gather your energy. As you do the movements, let your breathing be relaxed. Coordinate all the different parts of your body together so that each motion is a flow from the whole body. Make your motions continuous and slow. Keep your back relatively straight and hips shifting between your feet, sixty percent over the supporting foot, forty percent over the leading foot, then reversing as you step. Don't lean overly. Let your movements be rounded and natural. Keep in mind that the inner aspects of circulating energy and breathing should always be coordinated with the outer aspects of the motions.

The exercises that follow are a sampling of tai chi movements. If you like them, you can learn the complete set of exercises from many excellent books, videotapes, or at a tai chi class.

Preparation (Figures 35 and 36)

Stand with your feet shoulder-width apart and arms hanging loosely at your sides. Then raise your two hands, very slowly, with palms facing the floor as you inhale. Lift lightly until you reach shoulder height. Exhale and slowly lower your hands, as if pressing on a ball, until they are extended back down again, keeping palms facing downward.

Rollback and Press (Figures 37 and 38)

Shift slowly toward the left as you step out to the left side with your left foot into a left front stance, also known as the bow-and-arrow stance. At the same time, move your left hand forward, palm facing you, wrist and elbow slightly rounded. Pull your hands back as you simultaneously shift your weight over to the back foot. Then shift forward again over your front foot while you push your bent left arm with the right hand. Allow your whole body to move together. Try to be smooth and flowing in your movements. Repeat the sequence on the right side.

Rooster Stands on One Leg (Figures 39 and 40)

Step into a left front stance as you extend your left hand, palm facing toward you, arm extended, and right hand down at your side, palm facing down. Step up with your right leg, raising your knee as you move your right hand up and left hand down, then place your right

| Figure 35 | Figure 36 |

Preparation

foot down and repeat the pattern on the other side. Flow with your whole body moving in unison, relaxed, and balanced.

Pushing Hands
Pushing Hands is a two-person form of exercise performed in soft-style martial arts that teaches practitioners how to redirect force. It is a method for developing sensitivity and the ability to respond even to the subtlest cues. Practitioners learn to feel the opponent's force but not to oppose it. Instead, they gently follow and redirect it away so that they are not harmed, nor is the other person harmed. You may begin with one arm. There are many variations.

Figure 37

Figure 38

Rollback and Press

Figure 39

Figure 40

Rooster Stands on One Leg

Tao in Ten

Face your partner. Your partner extends one arm, slightly bent at the elbow, palm up. Extend your arm in a similar position and rest the back of your hand on top of your partner's, bent at the wrist. As your partner slowly moves his (or her) extended arm, you stick with it, (lightly) following the movement without interfering. As your partner twists and turns, continue to follow. Stay in touch with the back-and-forth rotation, remain relaxed, and do not interfere. This takes practice and mental alertness. If your concentration falters you may start pushing or pulling without realizing it. Roll back and forth together, taking turns as to who initiates the movement and who follows. Eventually try it with eyes closed.

A Modern Adaptation: Tae Chun Do

Tae chun do is a modern martial art that adapts Taoist principles. In this art, students learn that a punch is not merely a punch, nor is a block merely a block. Each technique has a profound meaning that generalizes into life. Learning this art is an inner journey that not only brings about competence in martial arts but also fosters competence in life.

Tae chun do trains students in both hard and soft force. They learn that even in the most forceful yang there is always a bit of soft yin, and so they practice relaxing as part of a motion and only tightening at the moment of focus. The opposite is true for soft techniques. Purely soft moves contain subtle yang, since the opponent's force may be ever so gently redirected. Opponents' force is used against them so that they will often be sent flying across the room after a tae chun do soft block.

The basis for these skills is sensitivity and Oneness with the opponent. Students become very aware of force, its qualities and direction. Then they can blend with it to appropriately neutralize or redirect it.

Meditation is a central part of the daily workout. Students learn how to relax using their minds to let go of inner tension. They practice focusing their energy, circulating it, and then putting it into their technique. Thus the power of this style comes from within, forging a strong, flexible body, mind, and spirit.

Tae Chun Do Wave Block (Figures 41–43)

Tae chun do draws the spirit of its technique from nature. The Wave Block uses the spirit of the ocean and the natural power of waves. It is actually a block and a sweep combined.

Begin by swinging the left foot around in a large circular motion as you swing your two arms across in the opposite direction. This yin-yang motion creates two counterforces that cause the opponent to be thrown. Next, pull your right foot forward so that you are standing in a shorter stance as you simultaneously bring your right hand across the front of your body, palm open for one wave block, immediately followed by a second wave block from the left hand. Movements should be round and flowing. Think of the motion of a wave and draw your inspiration for the dynamic spirit of this technique.

Learning to Feel and Use Your Energy

> Follow the flow
> It leads to the source
> Find the center
> Be One with the force
> —C. Alexander Simpkins

Students of these martial arts learn about force. They become sensitive to the energy within and around them and learn how to use it to help situations. They embark on an inner journey that develops the mind so that the practitioner can respond naturally, in tune with Tao.

As you read through the sections that follow, try to think about the principles on several levels. On the one hand, these are effective techniques for defending against an attack. But on a deeper level, you will see implications for life in general. Reflect on the thoughts that will invariably arise as you experiment with the principles.

Figure 41   Figure 42

Figure 43

Tae Chun Do Wave Block

Force Sensitivity

> After you have learned to interpret energy, the more you prac-
> tice, the better your skill will be, and by examining thoroughly
> and remembering silently, you will gradually reach a stage of
> total reliance on the mind.
>
> —Liang 1977, 44

Taoists do not believe in confronting force directly. In fact, the best
defense is don't be there. You can handle any force that confronts you
by becoming sensitive to the energy from that force, not by opposing
it. When you stubbornly take a stand against something, you can lose
touch with it, and so may become overwhelmed by it. Sensitivity to
force is a skill that can be learned and responds to practice. Your meditative awareness makes it possible. Begin with your own sensory
awareness and expand it outward.

Personal Sensitivity Meditation

Lie on the floor and close your eyes. Let your attention scan your body
sensations. Let go of any unnecessary tension. Feel your breathing and
allow it to be natural. When you feel relaxed, notice how your body
presses down on the floor. Can you feel the supportive force of the
floor pushing up on your body? If you feel yourself pushing down, try
to relax to the floor. Allow yourself to take the support of the floor and
lie effortlessly for several minutes.

Sensing Force Exercise

Find a small stone to use in your meditation. Lie down and place the
stone on your stomach or chest. Close your eyes and sense the weight
of the stone as it presses down on you. If it is a small stone, the sensation may be subtle.

Listening with the Skin

The ability to listen with the skin is very helpful in sensing the energy around you. Like a sixth sense, this uses a combination of sensory input with intuitive understanding. One of our teachers liked to wear a blindfold when doing his martial art so that he relied entirely on sensitivity. Healers and martial artists use this ability to help them know when things are happening in the body or in the environment around them.

Pay attention to your skin. Does it feel warm or cool? Do you feel the air? Notice your hands. Feel the sensation in the palms and backs of your hands. Is there a difference? Try not to label your experience—simply feel what you feel.

Evading Force

A Taoist sage was walking down the street toward her car late at night. Suddenly she felt an inner urge to cross the street, so she did. As she looked back to where she had just been walking, she saw a man step out of a building in an aggressive manner and yell at traffic. She continued along until she was well past the man and crossed back to continue on her way. Had she not sensed something, she might have had to deal with the man's hostility. By using her intuition she was able to avoid the force.

The first line of defense in a potentially dangerous situation is to sense it before it happens. Intuitive awareness taps into the Tao. When people ignore these intuitions a small problem can become a much larger one. Deal with situations when they are small.

The martial arts application of evasion is to practice stepping aside as a punch comes in. This can be practiced with a partner who attacks. The defender pays close attention to the incoming force, and times a quick step sideways at ninety degrees to the attack so that the punch slides past, completely missing the defender.

Yielding to Go with the Force

Surfers intuitively know about the Taoist Way of yielding. When trying to paddle out past the waves that break close to shore, surfers will either duck under the wave coming toward them or ride over it. By doing this, they avoid the tremendous force of the crashing waves. Once out far enough, the surfers watch for waves. When the right wave approaches, they begin to paddle toward shore to gain some speed. Then they can ride with the wave, yielding to the force and allowing it to carry them on a magnificent adventure. Going with the force allows for new possibilities.

The principle of yielding to the force has broad applications in many contexts of life. Parents intend for their children to develop their natural abilities. But sometimes parents try to make their children comply. In one typical family therapy situation, a child unwilling to do his homework wanted to play instead. The frustrated parents demanded that their son do his schoolwork. This resulted in a stubborn refusal and belligerence, followed by yelling—a very unproductive exchange. As this continued, the whole family felt angry and unhappy.

The Taoist solution is to yield. We advised the parents to turn work into play. When the child had a report to do for school, the parents rented a movie about the subject. They ate popcorn and watched together, making it an enjoyable experience. Later they went to a museum that displayed the topic. The museum visit became a fun-filled family excursion, a special occasion. The parents were able to guide the child to find enjoyment in learning and have a good time, too. Their son discovered his own motivation, brought about by accepting his natural motivation to be happy and redirecting it into a happy enjoyment of study. Tensions dissolved, the report got done, and family unity was restored.

Soft-style martial arts apply these skills. As a punch comes in, the martial artist evades slightly but also flows with the incoming force. Practitioners put up a block to a punch but exert no force. Instead, they redirect the flow of the force so it travels past them.

Yielding Exercises

This exercise illustrates the Taoist idea of yielding. When a force comes toward you, meet it with awareness and sensitivity, yielding just enough so that its power is neutralized.

Collect some stones of different sizes. Toss one of the stones you found up in the air and feel its force as you catch it. Try a heavier stone. The heavier the stone, the more you will feel it enter your hand. Experiment with letting your hand yield slightly as you catch the stone. Can you catch it so effortlessly that you dissipate the force of the stone as it enters your hand?

Redirecting the Force

Sometimes evading or yielding to a force is not possible. Perhaps the force is too great or you did not notice it until it was right in front of you. Taoists use their sensitivities to redirect the force just enough so that it changes direction and moves away.

The president of a business was having difficulty dealing with an employee who couldn't seem to do anything right. This worker tried hard but always made critical mistakes that were costing the company money. Rather than fire him, which was his first impulse, the president applied a Taoist solution. Realizing that everyone has natural abilities, he thought very carefully about this employee's talents. Then he redirected the man into a new position where he proved to be a valuable member of the staff.

If a difficult force or obstacle develops in your life, try redirecting it so that you are safe from its effects. Evade properly but do not lose touch in order to avoid.

When you are in tune with Tao and remain centered in yourself, you can make use of the natural yin-yang built into any situation. Remain in touch with others and the situation, and you can flow with harmony. Blending with the force, flowing with the cycles, you express your inner strength the Taoist Way.

Enhancing
Your Creativity

It is easy to appreciate the idea of Tao, but quite another matter
to give it form.

—from the *Mustard Seed Garden Manual* in Sze 1959, 128

Artistic Expression in Chinese Art

In China, Tao has been expressed through painting, sculpture, poetry,
calligraphy, music, architecture, and other arts. In architecture, for
example, Tao is expressed through the use of patterns and space. In
painting, Tao is expressed in the lines and patterns and in the blank,
unfilled areas between. The pigments used are often symbolic of the
Five Elements—earth is yellow, metal is gray, fire is red, water is blue,
and wood is greenish-brown.

Yin and yang are woven deeply into the fabric of Taoist art, sym-
bolized in various ways, which became accepted visual codes of meaning. As time passed, a traditional symbol might be reinterpreted but
never simply dismissed. For example, brush and ink are as yin and
yang. Ink is yin to the artist but yang to the paper, and in turn, ink is

Misty Evening, artist unknown. Qing dynasty, China. Ink on silk, hanging scroll.
San Diego Museum of Art.

yin to the artist's chi expressed as intention and perception of the landscape or event. Yin and yang flow back and forth. Brushstrokes evolved from the combination of technique with philosophy, of individual Tao with universal Tao.

Abstraction

Pure and eternal art is timeless. It gains in strength with the passage of time. True art resonates with everyone's spirit.

The great spokesman for abstract art Wassily Kandinsky said that the source of spiritual beauty in abstract art is whether it is harmonious or disharmonious. Furthermore, "The creation of a true work of art is a mystery beyond comprehension" (Kandinsky 1946, 94).

The inner spirit of art uses outer form to express itself. The inner life of the composition becomes the guide. The spirit of Chinese art comes from its unique use of abstraction drawn directly from Taoist principles. In Western tradition, we are accustomed to the notion of reasoning from the concrete to the abstract. We begin with an event, a person, or an object, and then abstract features and qualities to lead us to deductions concerning their meaning. For example, looking at a table in front of us, we may abstract key features from our perception or experience of it—it may be constructed of wood or stand at a certain height, with a shelf or a drawer. Any of these features is an abstraction from the total unity, the table. A table is more than just the sum of its features. Though it always includes these features, the central focus is the concrete object: the table.

To the Taoist, however, the table is a pattern, a unity of function, of use. A block of wood, a chair, anything can serve as a table depending on how it is used and our relationship to it. A boundary of "tableness" does not quite exist. At a certain point, a table may become a chair if someone sits on it. But Westerners might just think of themselves as sitting on a table. The object is real; its use is transitory. The reverse is true in Taoism: Use is real; objects are transitory.

All is in flux, changing. The artistic creation is gathered by abstraction. The abstraction, the momentary pattern of Tao, is the reality. This perspective guides Taoist artists and frees them to express the inner essence perceived in the momentary apparent object.

Use of Perspective

The use of centralized perspective in Chinese art is unique and expressive. The introduction of a vanishing-point perspective into Western art during the Renaissance marked significant progress in painting theory. But in Chinese painting, based in the harmonious unity of Tao, this kind of perspective has never been used, even today. Often, Chinese paintings put the viewer at a certain vantage point—for example, looking down from a mountaintop, or far away and blurred. Everything is presented together, as Oneness, from this perspective. During the Sung period, level distance where everything is the same was popular. This approach to perspective projects three-dimensional space on two-dimensional surfaces. These methods bring the spectator into the picture to share in Tao. We gaze at paintings from the Taoist frame of reference and find ourselves transformed into Tao.

The Taoist artist is a visionary, able to give an experience to the viewer through a few marks of ink on rice paper. The relationship of a work of art to the viewer, and the artist to creation, becomes part of the application of Tao. So in a way, chi from the artist activates the chi of the spectator, making this art form a way to communicate Taoist concepts.

Interplay of Technique and Tao

The famous guide for Chinese artists, *Mustard Seed Garden Manual of Painting*, describes how to do patterns of brushstrokes that suggest trees, bamboo, rocks, people, birds, and even plum blossoms. Patterns of ink strokes, colors, and shapes are used by the painter to express Tao, moved by chi, evoking perception in the viewer.

Traditional techniques of the brush can express flowing like water, or solid objects like a rock. And rocks may be painted in a way that

Mysterious Clouds Hover While Water Falls into the Blue Mountain, Ben-long Zhu.
Twentieth-century, China. Ink on rice paper, hanging scroll. Private collection.

seems to make them look fluid like water or vice versa. The "bones" of a tree may be painted like a skeleton, beneath a landscape; at other times, the trees, bamboos, plum blossoms, even people may be given a "boneless" fluid, cloudlike appearance. This aesthetic can be applied to poetry, to music, to sculpture, to architecture, and varied a great deal according to the artist's vision.

The "Six Canons of Painting" is included in the *Mustard Seed Garden Manual*. These six canons are the pillars of creative art from which traditional painters never depart. The first and most important canon derives directly from Taoism. It states "Chi Yun, Shen Tung," which means chi flows and spirit follows. Once in tune with Tao, the brush moves in tune with spirit. Thus the inner breathes life into form through action.

Chi Yun, Shen Tung Exercise

Go out in nature with the instruments of your art. If you are a painter, bring your paints; photographers, bring your cameras; writers, pen and paper. Find a place where the chi is flowing. This could be a place with a waterfall, a strong wind, or even a busy street corner. Ready your instruments and then wait until you feel the chi of the scene; let it move your artistic spirit to express it. The stroke or the words are less important than the chi that inspires it. This is the source of technique when you attune to the first canon.

From the Tao comes yin and yang, so to express Tao in artistic form evolves from yin and yang. Whatever you want to do in art, you may begin with the opposite. "If you aim to dispense with method, learn method. If you aim at facility, work hard. If you aim for simplicity, master complexity" (Sze 1959, 131).

Yin-Yang Exercise

Think about what you are trying to do with your art. You probably have pursued your goals with a passion and direction that has taken you well along. But you might gain new depth by experimenting with some of the Taoist methods. Let go of your goals for a moment, experiment with the opposite, whatever that is for you. Keep your mind and emotions open, allow yourself to grow. You may make new discoveries and gain new skills.

Enhancing Your Creativity

Creativity leads back to Tao, for Tao is the source of all creating, expressed as yin and yang, moving with chi. Individual creative works can help to point you to Tao: The act of creation is a way to be close to Tao. Tao goes from the uncreated to the created. When you create, you are tapping into the spirit of Tao.

The creative process, being close to Tao, shares many of the same characteristics, such as spontaneity and flexibility. If you develop your own spontaneity and flexibility, you can foster the natural flow of creation for you.

Spontaneity

I have said that poetry is the spontaneous overflow of powerful feelings; it takes its origins from emotion recollected in tranquility.

—Wordsworth in Ghiselin 1952, 84

The young, free-spirited Neo-Taoists interpreted classical Taoism in a new way. They lived according to Tao with passion and contentment, without being tied to the past. Spontaneity was one of the key elements in living their Taoist life, drawn from the classic tradition of Chuang-tzu.

Spontaneity is healthy. According to Dr. Adolf Meyer, the founder of psychobiology and a leading figure in early psychotherapy in America, the mark of mental health is spontaneity. He said, "It is spontaneity that I want to study and inquire into and cultivate and respect as the all-important quality of a person" (Meyer 1952, 464).

Spontaneity arises from within, from the deeper, emerging parts of our nature. As Meyer explained, "By the person's spontaneity, I mean that which the person may be expected to rise to and to rise with on his own" (Meyer 1952, 464). Developing your spontaneity will allow you to express who you are.

Spontaneous response is not patterned, predictable, or redundant. Like water, Tao takes on the shape and form of its temporary expression, but pour it out, empty the cup, and water becomes formless, shapeless, flowing once more. So spontaneous response is usually in relation to a situation, a context, or a perception, but not determined by it. The container is the form that holds the water of Tao. It is not the water of Tao. Confusion of form with content is common. Spontaneity makes life interesting and always new. Water can be in a multitude of shapes, depending on the container's form.

Balance

In keeping with the Taoist principles of yin-yang balance, true spontaneity never loses sight of balance. Spontaneous does not need to mean without any connection to anything tangible or reasonable. You can allow spontaneous impulse to emerge in response to circumstances and follow it, without losing the center of life in Tao. In this way, you can flow with impulse, inner feelings, and needs without being swept away by them. When you are in tune with Tao, you know when to begin and when to end.

The story of the Neo-Taoist Wang Hui-chih illustrates this point. Awakened from a deep sleep, Wang felt a strong spontaneous impulse to visit his friend Tai. Even though it was a long journey, he decided to follow his impulse and left his house. He boarded an all-night boat that would take him close to Tai's home. But just as he walked up the walkway to Tai's door, he abruptly turned around and went home. Later, one of Wang's friends asked him why he had not followed through with the visit. Wang explained without hesitation, "I came on the impulse of my pleasure, and it is ended, so I go back. Why should I see Tai?" (Fung Yu-Lan 1966, 236).

It may seem like a contradiction to try to be deliberately spontaneous, but you can set the stage. The following two exercises encourage the conditions in which spontaneous responses tend to happen. If you would like to open up the possibility, experiment and enjoy the results.

Exercise in Following Spontaneity

Spontaneity evolves from an unplanned impulse, but it also involves sensitivity to that impulse. Sit quietly and close your eyes. Let yourself relax for a few minutes and do nothing. Eventually a desire to do or think something will arise within. Let it emerge and try to be aware of it as it arises. If the desire seems like a positive one, act on it. For example, you may feel like shifting your position, or perhaps you remember you forgot to make a telephone call.

Spontaneity One with Tao Exercise

The Taoist idea of spontaneity is to remain in tune with Tao. Then your spontaneous desire or impulse will always be the best one, taking you in a productive, positive direction. This exercise is designed to attune you to the larger perspective. Keep the whole in mind, so that you don't lose sight of the Tao of your whole being and all you are meant to do in your life to fulfill your destiny.

Clear your mind and relax quietly. Wait for an impulse to emerge but allow yourself to be aware of the broader context. For example, if your desire is to relax by reading a book but you have to be at work in an hour, keep the greater whole in mind. Usually your impulse alters naturally to reflect the greater Tao. When you attune to your spontaneous impulse within the Tao, you can sense whether you want to read and then go to work, or whether you can stay home and unwind, without interfering with your Tao of work.

Developing Flexibility the Taoist Way

An important step on the Taoist path to spontaneity is learning how to be flexible. The famous psychoanalyst Lawrence Kubie believed that flexibility is spontaneous and essential for creativity.

> The measure of health is flexibility, the freedom to learn through experience, the freedom to change with changing internal and external circumstances, to be influenced by reasonable argument, admonitions, exhortation, and the appeal to emotions; the freedom to respond appropriately to the stimulus of reward and punishment, and especially the freedom to cease when sated. The essence of normality is flexibility in all these vital ways. (Kubie 1961, 20)

A flexible, relaxed mind can help to foster a flexible, relaxed body just as a flexible, relaxed body will help to bring about a relaxed, calm mind. Mind and body are One. These exercises will help you develop more inner and outer flexibility and relaxation.

A body that is flexible and soft allows chi to flow freely. "Can you concentrate your vital force (chi) and achieve the highest degree of weakness like an infant?" (*Tao Te Ching* 10, in Chan 1963, 144). Bending like the willow when a forceful wind blows through a forest, the flexible trees will survive, while the big strong oak inevitably must reach its breaking point and snap in two.

Lao-tzu encourages us to be flexible in order to live life most fully:

> Soft and bending is the way of the living;
> Hard and brittle is the way of the dying.
> (*Tao Te Ching* 76, Grigg 1995, 52)

Practice of martial arts and chi kung will help you become more flexible. If you are not a martial artist or if you would like to enhance the process, these exercises can help you take a Taoist approach to relaxation.

Wu-Wei Relaxation

Taoism encourages us to be loose and flexible on the one hand, while also advising us not to *try* to do anything. This may seem like a paradox—to be relaxed without trying to be relaxed—but actually it is possible. We all have a built-in ability to be relaxed. The trick is to know how to trigger this natural ability.

Everyone has times when they feel relaxed. For some people, reading a good book is relaxing; while others find vigorous exercise makes them feel calm.

Sit quietly in a comfortable place. Close your eyes. Think about a time when you felt very relaxed. Perhaps you were on vacation or simply enjoying some time with friends or family. Vividly recall the experience. Remember the details—perhaps the aroma of a delicious meal or a lush flower garden, the repetitive sounds of waves breaking on the sandy shore, or wind rustling through the trees, or maybe the warmth of good company. As you think about this experience, your body will naturally relax.

You can learn to call upon your natural ability to relax whenever you want by simply inviting the response to happen. Experiment and you will discover your own ways of relaxing without trying to relax.

Natural Relaxation Response

This exercise utilizes the natural capacity of the body to tense some muscles while others are loose during certain movements. When you lift your arm, for example, the front of your arm is tense, but the back of the arm is loose.

Raise your arm and hold it up in the air until you feel tired. Then lower your arm and let the muscles relax of themselves. Explore other motions.

Yin-Yang Relaxation

You can learn about something by exploring what it is not. By becoming aware of how you tense, you will find yourself able to be naturally relaxed.

Lie on your back on the floor. If the floor is uncomfortable, use a couch or a bed. Close your eyes. Make fists with your hands and tighten them for about thirty seconds. Notice how the muscles feel when they are tight. Sense how long your arms are. Now open your fists and relax both arms. Feel your muscles let go. How long do your arms feel now? Compare the sensations with how you felt when you were tensing. Become aware of the quality in your arms when you are not tensing.

Next, tighten your neck and face. Scrunch your eyes tightly shut, tighten every part of these areas and hold for thirty seconds. Notice how you tighten these muscles. Then let go and totally relax for thirty seconds. Notice the difference.

Move through your body, part by part—back, chest, and pelvis, then legs and feet—first tightening and then relaxing. Try to keep the other parts relaxed and concentrate on one section at a time.

Finally, tighten your entire body at once for thirty seconds and then let go of all tensing. Stay with the relaxation for several minutes. Let your awareness scan through your body. Do you notice any tightness anywhere? Can you feel yourself clenching these muscles? Try to let go of any unnecessary tensing and allow yourself to be fully relaxed.

Practice this exercise over several days and you will become more familiar with how you tighten and relax your muscles. This awareness will help you to gain the ability to allow not tightening.

Not-Tightening Awareness

When people are going through their day, they often waste energy with unnecessary tension. You can change these unconscious patterns by taking an inward glance here and there to observe your muscle tension. Are you holding your jaw tight? Are your shoulders raised? Once you become aware of tension in an area, can you gently let go to allow the muscles to become looser, more naturally at ease? Take a glance in all kinds of situations and you will learn about yourself.

Stretching the Taoist Way

Stretching properly can develop flexibility. Taoists believe in starting small, and this philosophy applies well to stretching. As science learns more about the human body, the importance of a gentle stretching has become evident (Simpkins 1993, 33–38). Less is more, as Taoism claims. When people try to force their muscles to stretch, the opposite occurs—the muscle responds by tightening more.

Approach stretching with a relaxed mind. Sit quietly for a few minutes to allow your thoughts to settle. This calm mental attitude will spread naturally throughout your body. Then begin doing the stretches you like to do. But do them slowly and gently. Listen to what your body tells you through the sensations such as comfort and pain. Your muscles will let you know when they are ready for a longer extension by releasing without discomfort.

Stretch regularly. Properly stretched on a regular basis, your muscles will let go of their habitual excess tension. You are never too young or too old to become more flexible. Being flexible will help your chi to flow without obstruction or blockage. When you can be spontaneous and flexible, you will be more open and responsive to the chi around you. Then you can draw inspiration from your environment at every turn.

Pure Conversation

Creativity does not have to be confined to making an art object. You can be creative in every aspect of your life. Even the most basic activities of life offer opportunities to express yourself.

As early as Lao-tzu, Tao was interpersonal, shared values and ways of experiencing. You do not just have to sit quietly to experience Tao, though this is one way and a good beginning. As you grow in your understanding of Tao, you share it and affect others with it, as others affect you with Tao's flowing nature.

Conversation is a lost art, but it can be revitalized the Taoist way. Conversation defines us and our reality. We create and evoke a shared world in our conversations, or communicate our shared world. We know it is important to talk, and important to be silent.

Have you ever had a conversation, deep into the evening, with a friend, a loved one, or even a person you recently met with whom you can relate and communicate deeply about life, meaning, and reality? On and on you talked, into the abyss of time, until the world as you shared it together became clear, and you felt at peace with it. This is a conversational moment of the Tao of shared meaning.

The Neo-Taoists made conversation part of their system, faithfully sharing dialogues about truth, wisdom, and understanding. In the Pure Conversation School, Neo-Taoists reinterpreted classical Taoism as a way to live with passion and contentment in accord with Tao. They tried to be authentically true to themselves and each other, allowing their true nature to spontaneously emerge.

The French existentialist philosopher Gabriel Marcel pointed out that being present with others in dialogue leads to a mutual participation in a world of meaning, releasing us from ourselves, from preoccupation with ourselves. Other people can help us be in tune with great wisdom.

> Personal self-creation involves an openness to transcendent, suprapersonal reality in which the person is ultimately fulfilled. It involves self-consecration and self-sacrifice to something beyond oneself—a "creative fidelity" to being.
>
> —Cain 1963, 81

Faithfulness to ourselves and others is part of authentic existence. But it matters how fully we are ourselves. Truth in dialogue opens the doors of possibility. Conversation pursued deeply and sincerely may bring us to the path, may open the doors of perception.In dialogue, when people share their meanings, they gain the potential for a moment of mutual oneness with Tao. Life and other people are moments of self-expression of Tao.

In conversation, with true person-to-person dialogue, you can follow the Tao. Opportunity abounds to express the Tao paradoxically, by being at ease and comfortable. Letting be—that is, letting go of concern—may be interpreted as being in touch with one's feelings and sentiments, of letting them pass, in calmness.

Letting be can be expressed in conversation and can lead to positive virtues. Love, benevolence, and kindness are the response to others. Let the situation be. The little child, innocent and open to others, is the ideal state to be in, to express Tao.

Your Pure Conversation

To engage in the spirit of Tao, just like the Neo-Taoists did so many years ago, allow yourself to engage in a pure conversation with someone—someone you know well or someone you don't know at all if this is appropriate. Engage deeply, be authentically yourself, less inhibited, without extremes or compulsion. Let yourself be spontaneous at times. Follow the flow of the conversation to its roots.

Conversation is creation in motion. As you allow yourself to engage in creative conversation, to become interested in other people, you learn about yourself and your world. You expand outward to universal Tao.

Follow Your Dreams

Although the Tao is simple,
It cannot be explained.
Because it cannot be explained,
No one can understand it.
If people would follow
Its simple way,
The natural rhythms of all things
Would rise and fall in easy order.
—*Tao Te Ching* 32, Grigg 1995, 101

Taoism encourages an unconscious, trance orientation to life. Using your unconscious as reference may seem very different from the typical Western approach, but you will be surprised what a positive resource your unconscious mind can be. When you use your unconscious and stop trying to do everything with your conscious mind, you will be naturally attuned to Tao.

The Unconscious Mind

We are accustomed to using our conscious mind. It is what we use to define the world, make distinctions, and think deliberately. Our conscious knows what we are thinking and we make our choices based on these deliberate thoughts.

The unconscious is different. Unconscious perception occurs outside of awareness, so what the unconscious perceives and what it processes happens without conscious recognition. People know something without knowing how they know it. Taoists seek no-knowledge in order to open the gates to unconscious perception, to bring them closer to Tao.

Not the Freudian Unconscious

> To Freud, the unconscious was a product of consciousness, and the unconscious simply contained the remnants of consciousness; I mean that he saw the unconscious as a sort of storeroom where all the discarded things of consciousness were heaped up and left. To me, however, the unconscious was a matrix, a sort of basis of consciousness, possessing a creative nature and capable of autonomous acts . . .
>
> —Carl Jung in Evans 1981, 134

The unconscious that Taoism refers to is not quite the same as the Freudian idea of the unconscious. Freud viewed the unconscious as a storehouse, the reservoir of repressed forces in conflict. The symbolic imagery of dreams is the path to the Freudian unconscious. Freudian analysis seeks to make their meaning conscious, thereby freeing people from their conflicts.

By contrast, Taoism does not encourage analyzing unconscious symbols to make them conscious. Taoists consider the unconscious a positive resource for enriching and enhancing our lives. We should use trance instead of rational thought to tap into this resource and bring us closer to Tao. The conflicts and problems that Freud attributed to unconscious forces are actually imagined conflicts that come from the rational mind. By returning to the natural source within, we can open new potentials and bypass problems without effort.

Unconscious Intelligence

Taoism has long claimed that the unconscious has its own intelligence, drawn directly from the wisdom of Tao. It takes in information, thinks, and draws conclusions. Sometimes the solution seems to appear mysteriously. This is because intuition often occurs backward—as if we know the answer before the question, but the final result makes sense. Our hypnosis teacher, Milton H. Erickson, M.D., shared the Taoist idea of unconscious wisdom. He liked to tell people, "Your unconscious is a lot smarter than you are!"

Modern psychology has shown that the unconscious mind can know things that the conscious mind misses. Psychologist J. A. Groeger did a very interesting experiment that showed this clearly (Groeger, 1984). He flashed words on a screen. Half the subjects received the words faster than they could consciously perceive them, registering them unconsciously. The second group had the words flashed a little slower, so they were consciously aware of seeing the words. Later, all subjects were given a list of words and asked to pick the ones they had seen on the screen. The list did not actually have the words flashed on the screen but it did contain words that were similar in meaning or sound.

The results were surprising. Conscious perception proved to be more superficial than unconscious perception. When the word *town*, for example, was flashed, unconscious perceivers picked "city," showing that they understood the meaning. The consciously perceiving subjects missed the meaning entirely: They picked "time," a word that sounded similar.

Unconscious Freedom

The unconscious mind is the source of freedom. Dr. Erickson believed that the unconscious bypasses limitations about what we can and cannot do. Erickson often worked with patients to help them reclaim freedom from these limits through hypnotic trance (Erickson and Rossi, 1980).

The Taoists also recognized that the unconscious allows people to be free. Lieh-tzu told this story of a middle-aged man named Yang-li who suffered from severe memory loss. Anything that happened in the morning he forgot by the evening. At any moment he could not remember what had just happened. His family was very upset and called in a doctor to help.

By the end of the treatment Yang-li's memory was restored. But then he became very angry. He yelled at his wife, beat his sons, and chased the doctor wielding a weapon. When the police arrested him, they asked him to explain why he was so angry.

"When my memory was impaired, I was unconscious of the external world. I was at peace. Now, worry, insecurity, and all kinds of emotions put me in turmoil. Oh, if I could reclaim my oblivion!" (paraphrased from Giles 1959, 65–66).

We may not want the extreme memory loss of Yang-li, but the story illustrates the value of being able to let go of the previous moment and simply experience each thing as it is. Sometimes, too much consciousness leads to negative consequences.

Unconscious Trance Meditation

Trance is an altered state of consciousness that lets you bypass the conscious mind and open unconscious perception. If you would like to experience trance, try this exercise. Do this exercise at home, where you can be at ease.

Wait until you have some free time with no responsibilities to attend to. Find a quiet place where you can be undisturbed for fifteen minutes or more. Sit or lie down so that you can be comfortable.

You can find your way into your first trance by looking at an interesting object. Look at the object carefully. Study it, noticing all its components, colors, and shapes. Next, look at the outline, then the interior. Focus all your attention on the object. As you concentrate fully, your thoughts will drift. Let your body relax, your breathing rate settle. As you continue to observe the object, can you see any alterations in it? For example, you may see blurring, a change in color, or an alteration in shape. How does the object appear to change? Be curious to experience and wait for your response.

Seek-the-Image-Within Trance

You might like to try this exercise after the previous one. As you are looking at your chosen object, imagine your eyelids becoming heavy. Let them become heavier and heavier until they want to close. If they don't want to close after a little time, simply close them gently. Relax your eyelids and allow your entire body to completely relax.

It is possible to visualize color in a formless, abstract, or symbolic manner. At first the color may appear as just a shade. Gradually it could alter in its depth or even change colors. Sometimes people see a kaleidoscope of color. Other times it is simply white or black afterimages, lights, or streaks. Experiment with offering a suggestion for a color you would like to experience. Wait for your response and allow it to evolve.

When you feel ready, allow all your sensations to return to normal, refreshed and alert.

Tranquillity Trance

Taoists learn to become absolutely tranquil, like a still pond that reflects without a single ripple. Sit quietly and comfortably. Let your body relax and your breathing become regular. Set aside your usual concerns; temporarily forget about your difficulties. Do not think about anything in particular except to wonder how quiet you could be. Sometimes it is helpful to remember a time when you felt peaceful.

Allow your muscles to relax and let your mind be tranquil. Suggest to yourself that if your unconscious would like, you could become completely still, like the pond. From this clear, calm trance you are One with Tao.

When you feel ready, count backwards from five to one, letting your sensations gradually return to normal, until you are fully awake and alert.

Life Is But a Dream

Taoists apply unconscious functioning broadly. Not only should people forget things and events, but they should also forget themselves. By letting go of your personal ego you can be unconscious at the most profound level, freeing you to tap into your vast unconscious potential.

One of the most famous illustrations of this came from Chuang-tzu. One night, Chuang-tzu dreamt he was a butterfly, fluttering freely, happy and content, doing exactly what he wanted. He didn't know he was Chuang-tzu. Suddenly he awoke and realized he was definitely a man. But he didn't know if he was Chuang-tzu who had dreamt he was a butterfly, or a butterfly dreaming he was a man!

Accepting Your Dreams

People often realize that they are having a dream when something bizarre or impossible is happening in the dream, such as being able to fly (LaBerge 1985). Usually, they try to test reality by recognizing that what is happening in the dream is impossible. This is helpful if the dream is frightening.

But Taoism encourages us not to be frightened. Try to accept this nonreality as an interesting, mind-expanding experience. You can grow from your dream experiences through unconscious learning. So if, for example, you dream you are a butterfly dreaming you are a person, and you experience yourself as a butterfly, you might learn something new from a butterfly's perspective. Perhaps you would understand more about freedom and spontaneity, or become aware of things not readily understood by rational analysis. Be a butterfly, learn its perspective.

Exercise to Accept Your Dream

This exercise will help you to use your dreams as the Taoists do, to learn more about yourself and expand your perspective.

Try to be aware of your dream while you are dreaming. At the same time, allow yourself to be immersed in the experience, to live it. Let yourself make any new associations that occur to you, either while sleeping or later when you wake up. Be open to new thoughts.

Dreams Are Important

When we are asleep, it is not just a matter of turning off a switch. During sleep we go through a rich set of stages that activate many parts of the brain. Dreams are the most notable part of sleep and are to some degree a part of every night's sleep.

Sleep research is being conducted in sleep laboratories around the world in an attempt to try to understand more about sleeping and dreaming. Volunteers allow themselves to be observed and tested during and following sleep. Although Western scientists are certain that we need sleep, they are still trying to understand why (Farthing 1992). Taoists, on the other hand, accept the unknown and work with it.

Being awake and being asleep are two sides of life. Each serves an important purpose. The Taoists gave sleep and dreaming equal importance to waking. In one Taoist story, a wealthy man treated his elderly servant very badly. He worked him so hard that each night the poor servant fell asleep utterly exhausted. Yet he was a happy man. A friend asked him how he could possibly be happy with such a hard life. The servant replied, "Every night I dream I am a king, ruling a large kingdom and living luxuriously in a beautiful palace. Since life is equally divided between waking and sleeping, why should I complain when half my life is perfect!"

Meanwhile, the wealthy man fell into a troubled sleep each night, worrying about his responsibilities. Every night he dreamt that he was a servant, suffering under the unmerciful demands of a cruel master. He slept so poorly that he eventually became ill. A friend advised him, "You have achieved much in your life, but your dreams seem to reflect the proper balance of your destiny." The man recognized the wisdom in these words, and in response lightened his servant's load and treated him with kindness. In time the wealthy man began to worry less. His dreams improved and he became a much happier man.

Why Dreams Are Important

The Taoists explain why dreams are just as important as waking. They claim both are equally real and unreal, that all is in transition: People are on this earth for a borrowed amount of time. Nothing lasts forever, and in this sense, nothing is real. Taoists consider it cause for rejoicing. Since everything is a passing illusion, a dream can have just as much reality as the real world. Therefore, we can benefit from our dreams just as we benefit from real-life experience.

Tapping Unlimited Potentials

Dreams, being unconscious, have no limit. In dreams you are not constrained by gravity, the seasons, where you live, or what you do. In the dream state you can soar in the Heavens and be completely free. Taoist sages, who were comfortable shifting between conscious and unconscious states, could do anything. They could walk through walls and fly in the sky and roam freely between dreams and reality.

Sages used dreams to free themselves and those they advised to let go of limits in life by looking at things from a new perspective. Many teaching stories show the therapeutic use of dreams to help people transcend their everyday perspective and discover new possibilities.

For fifteen years, the Yellow Emperor enjoyed ruling his country, gratifying all his desires and seeking pleasure whenever he could. But for the next fifteen years he grew bored and depressed, dull and confused. He withdrew from ruling for three months. During this time he lived simply, away from all pressure. One day he fell asleep and dreamt he journeyed to a kingdom far away. This country had no ruler and yet the people were happy and fulfilled. When he awoke, he returned to his country and called in his ministers. "Now I understand that the Way must be discovered from within each person. I can't impose it on others."

For twenty-eight more years he ruled his country in this way. By facilitating instead of dominating, he was much more effective. His kingdom flourished almost as much as the dream-kingdom. When he died, his people mourned him for two hundred years, and he is still remembered today as one of China's great rulers.

Dreams teach you things about yourself and your future. By accepting the dream state as a valid aspect of your life, you can expand your conception of reality and your own capacities.

To the Taoists, dreams have the power to help you transform. In the West, we have also thought that dreams hold the key to inner change. Psychoanalysis analyzes the symbols in dreams as reflections of the unconscious mind, resulting in deeper personal understanding. By experiencing a significant dream people are changed.

A long trip can also have a transformative effect. When you return home you may suddenly notice something you hadn't seen before—a different way to live, perhaps, or new possibilities. Taoists use dreams in a very similar way. Story after story tells of Taoist sages taking a person on a dreamlike voyage to a new and often mystical place. Upon their return, the student has gained a new perspective. Small-minded concerns don't feel the same. The beauty and wonder of life as it is opens up. The student has grown wiser, not by rational thought but from unconscious understanding.

Exercise in Dream Learning
You can use Taoist dream learning to transcend your own limits and make new discoveries by floating your perspective, as Chuang-tzu did

as a butterfly. This exercise is drawn from the methods used by Taoist sages who encouraged their students to use their inborn ability to dream and imagine as tools for personal development.

A good time to try this is just as you fall asleep or right after you awake, because at these times you are in the twilight state between waking and dreaming. Make yourself comfortable, either sitting or lying down. Here are some suggestions, though you may want to think of your own.

Imagine that you are old and wise. Allow a picture of yourself to form but don't push it. Let your unconscious mind come up with ideas. What do you understand looking back at yourself today?

Imagine that you are a young child, carefree and happy. What are you like? Try to think of some situations.

Take a journey to a wonderful place where everything is ideal. What is this place like? Wander through and notice what you see.

When you open your mind to the wisdom of your unconscious you will find it helping you both day and night. Your unconscious is a positive part of you, always there if you are willing to recognize it. Listen to your intuitions. Allow yourself to be open to a vague thought that may even seem illogical at first. The unconscious offers flickers that can be recognized by the conscious mind. As you become more receptive to your unconscious, you open the pathway of communication that becomes easier to receive. You will be rewarded with fulfilling insights and understandings leading to Tao.

From Tao to Te

Mastering Life

> The greatest power
> exercises no power.
> The greatest strength
> arises from humility.
> The greatest virtue
> follows the way of the Tao
> —*Tao Te Ching* 68, Grigg 1995, 44

When Tao is applied in the real world, it is expressed as Te, a kind of power, a fullness of being. Tao leads to a new perspective for action. How can you act? You act by nonaction. Tao is the criterion, the standpoint to use as your basis. Not by contrast, not by opposition, but by relation to unity with the Way.

Te is the natural by-product of following the Path. Staying with Tao gives you a certain kind of power, a power to influence that happens spontaneously and moves in tune with the forces that are already

141

there. But this power is not imposed from without. Instead, influence comes from within, self-regulating.

To express your Te, you facilitate this self-regulating natural process by stepping back, not by imposing your will, personal intention, or code of conduct. These qualities arise naturally when you are sensitive to your unconscious mind and allow your true nature to flourish of itself. Farmers fertilize crops to help them grow, but they can't make their crops grow taller or quicker by pulling on them. Plants need correct conditions, rooted in the ground of their being. Similarly with your Te. Cultivate your sensitivity to the needs of situations. Like the farmer who knows not to overwater or overfertilize, you don't ignore the natural rhythms of care needed. Sensitize yourself to the cycles of the universe to better serve its needs. Your Te develops and its influence follows, but do not try to control with it.

The Unity of Tao: Balance Beyond Conflict

Tao is in a continual relationship with the actual world. Through flux and change, the Tao relates. Reversion is the Law of Tao, it reverts and switches, so the old expression "What goes around, comes around" is not just interpersonal destiny but internal, too.

This perspective results in a certain balance and stability no matter how the situations of life challenge you. You may at times be drawn into an opposing side, one of the dualities, but this is only temporary. The balance will return if you return to center.

We are used to either/or thinking. We conceive our dramas as good guys versus bad guys, love versus hate. But ultimately the higher synthesis brings a new perspective. The complexity of life transcends duality, even though it is expressed in polarity. When you return to the center, you can perceive both sides and can continue the process of change and flow.

Ripples from our deeds
glide over the ponds
of life once done,
to influence others
we cannot know
what they become
—C. Alexander Simpkins

Te Overcomes Conflict

Te evolves from trust in the Tao. When you have Te, you can resolve difficulties without fighting. If you are in conflict with another person or yourself, you cannot avoid it. Only when you face it and embrace it can you resolve it. Love and compassion combined with courage lead to success. Great leaders don't gain influence by being negative, aggressive, and hostile. They lead with love, trust, caring, and humility. According to Lao-tzu, taking this Path leads to great rewards. Everyone gains.

I have three treasures
that I treasure and guard.
The first is called "love";
the second is called "sufficiency";
the third is called "not daring to lead the world."
Through love one may be courageous,
through sufficiency one may be generous . . .
Whom Heaven wants to save
him he protects through love.
—*Tao Te Ching*, 58, Wilhelm 1990, 67

Don't quarrel angrily. Hostility won't lead to any positive result. Be tranquil, in harmony with circumstances, and things work out. Chi will flow on its winding path. The forces of change are continuous and unceasing. Trust these forces. Be patient, stay with the flow and let it be. Try to impede the flow and you will be swept away by it.

Aggression breeds further aggression; it elicits its reciprocal, and consequences will follow until the balance is restored, as it must be. Domination inevitably brings about a reaction to it, not just peaceful submission. Newton's law states that every force elicits an equal and opposite counterforce. If you push a compression spring down and release, it springs back with an opposite force. Don't engage in the one lest you provoke the other.

When a person is hostile and aggressive, he creates a potential for reciprocation, a duality that balances the forces. But the reciprocation will not be linear—it is circular. The other person may not become aggressive back; she may become hostile to a third party. Many other consequences can follow. The relationship is complex. Therefore, even in the heat of battle, strikes against the enemy should be made with regret and benevolence, not hostility. There is no joy in conquest; it is an occasion for sorrow.

When you express your Te, you reach for a higher synthesis, beyond the dualities, beyond the conflict. This relationship to a higher principle requires a certain tolerance for the unknown, for uncertainty and ambiguity, as well as faith that something higher is there. Since the higher principle transcends either side, it may not seem to make sense at first. But transcendence is central—balancing perspectives together, resolving them in a higher synthesis.

Meditation on Overcoming Conflict

Think about a conflict you are having, then consider the cycles of change and flow. Don't resist them. Open your heart compassionately. What is an opposite possibility? Can you think of a higher synthesis? By trusting the absolute, you become free of external influences, no longer reacting to problematic moments by struggle and opposition. Trust in the Tao. This applies to creative efforts as well as interpersonal concerns.

Now, let be. Allow yourself to relax for a few minutes, clear your mind of thoughts. Be tranquil and calm.

Skillful Living

I don't love working—it is working well that I love.

—Krenov 1976, 60

Te is expressed in skill, often unconscious. You just do it. You have probably had moments in your life when you did something exceptionally well. Without thinking about it, it just happened. This was a moment of Te. When you follow the Way you can perform with skill. At that moment you are attuned to the deeper essence, Tao.

Unfortunately, these moments of perfect skill may not happen very often. Frequently the problem is that we get in our own way. Many great athletes attest to the importance of being able to perform without thought, to allow their bodies to do what they have been trained to do. Here Taoism shares a similar idea with Zen Buddhism, as Eugen Herrigel describes a moment of Te:

> This state in which nothing definite is thought, planned, striven for, desired or expected, which aims in no particular direction and yet knows itself capable alike of the possible and the impossible, so unanswering is its power. (Herrigel 1971, 41)

Chuang-tzu talked about an archery contest where people were betting on the winner. When the stakes were small, everyone shot with skill. When stakes went higher, participants worried about their aim. When betting was for real gold, players became nervous and skill levels dropped. In all three cases the players' abilities remained the same, but because one prize meant more than another, people let these external conditions weigh on their mind, interfering with their performance. "He who looks too hard at the outside gets clumsy on the inside" (Chuang-tzu in Watson 1968, 201).

Milton Erickson once trained a professional golfer to use self-hypnosis to help combat the nervousness that increased hole-by-hole during a tournament. He taught the golfer to forget the score and to not know what hole he was playing. At the next tournament, the golfer teed up at the first hole with perfect confidence. He continued to play through the course without faltering. After the eighteenth hole, much to the surprise of the spectators and his caddy, the golfer took his ball and teed up again. He had played each hole as if it were the first, so of course he did not know when the game was over! Without any mental worry to get in the way, the golfer was able to play his best, with Te.

Exercise in Skillful Acts
Pick an activity in which you have developed some skill. It could be an art such as woodworking, painting, sculpting; or a physical skill such as tennis, golf, martial art; or even a skill in a game like chess, darts, backgammon. Whatever skill you choose, make it one that you have practiced many times.

Clear your mind and do not think about anything. Sit for several minutes and do one of the meditations from this book to quiet yourself. When you feel ready, begin the activity. For example, if you are playing darts, focus on the movement of your hand and arm, feel the dart in your hand and the flow of your movement. Do not fill your thoughts with "bull's-eye" or points; let the dart fly of itself. Your natural ability to hit the mark will be free to express itself without any mental doubts or worries to interfere.

Craftsmanship develops in this way. The craftsman trains and learns. This part is essential: to fully commit yourself to the learning process. As you begin to gain some skill, you can set knowledge aside and allow your natural instincts to be your guide.

With the years of training behind them, craftsmen can set aside their ego and allow themselves to be inspired by the work.

Khing, the master carver, made a bell stand
Of precious wood. When it was finished,
All who saw it were astounded. They said it must be
The work of spirits.
The Prince of Lu said to the master carver:
"What is your secret?"
Khing replied: "I am only a workman"
I have no secret. There is only this:
When I began to think about the work you commanded
I guarded my spirit, but did not expend it
On trifles that were not to the point.
I fasted in order to set
My heart at rest.
After three days fasting,
I had forgotten gain and success
After five days
I had forgotten praise or criticism
After seven days I had forgotten my body
With all its limbs.
By this time all thought of your Highness
And of the court had faded away
All that might distract me from the work
Had vanished . . .

What happened?
My own collected thought
Encountered the hidden potential in the wood.
From this live encounter came the work
Which you ascribe to the spirits."

      —Chuang-tzu in Krenov 1976, 7

Master woodcrafter James Krenov believes that a large part of craftwork has evolved from making a living to being a way of living (Krenov 1979, 9). The Way is primary: Doing something well is more a matter of attuning and sensing than anything else.

Even though the craftsman may create complex objects, simplicity is the guide. "We must be able to do the complex well, and yet arrive at, and preserve, simplicity" (Krenov 1979, 23). The Tao is simple, and the craftsman is one with Tao.

Attuned to Tao, craftsmen carefully sense their material. Woodworkers learn to know wood and its ways. They learn that the tree grows up and out, giving the grain in the wood a particular direction. Fine woodworkers attune sensitively to their wood. They run their hand along the grain and feel a difference—only one way follows the direction of the grain, like fur on a cat. Sanding and planing must be in harmony with this natural direction or else the wood grain will tear and scratch.

Craftsmen learn not to rush, to allow the work to take the time it needs to be done well. Similar to how tai chi practitioners never rush through their movements, the craftsman knows the price paid by impatience: mistakes. Although master craftsmen never hurry, they move with sureness.

Chuang-tzu described a butcher, Cook Ting, who could cut meat off the bones without ever needing to sharpen his knife. This was because he was so exact and perfect in his strokes that he never hit anything hard. He knew exactly where to cut and did so with exactness every time.

He explained how he was able to do this. He said that all he really cared about was the Way, which is beyond skill. When he first started to carve oxen, he only looked at the ox itself. After three years of continuous practice, he no longer saw the entire ox. Now he approached cutting with his spirit, never really looking with his eyes. Thinking stopped and spirit moved where it wanted to. He followed this natural

Teak and rosewood side table crafted by C. Alexander and Annellen Simpkins, inspired by their teacher James Krenov.

flow, slashing the large spaces and guiding the knife through the openings, following things just as they were.

He continued, explaining that when a cut became difficult, he would slow down, pay very close attention, and be sensitive to exactly what he was doing. In this way his knife stayed as sharp as his skill. Lord Weh-hui, on hearing Cook Ting's words, said, "I have heard your words and learned how to live my life!"

Living True to Your Nature, Expressing Your Te

Te is the actualization of Tao in the world. Taoists are concerned with the real world, and following the Way shows you how to live. Therefore you express yourself through Te. Everything compounds together in life: chi, shen (spirit), jing (essence), yin and yang. All are part of Tao, expressed as Te.

There is a unity, a Oneness. The world exists, but it finds expression through letting your true nature unfold, being who you are. By letting be, all comes to be. Take an attitude that allows you to spontaneously follow the Path you are on and to be facilitated by the natural forces that are inevitably present. As the woodworker expresses Te by crafting with exacting precision, you can express your Te through doing what you are given to do. Transcend every situation as it transcends you.

However complex or stressful your life is, it is all part of the Way. Step on the Path and you will find happiness and fulfillment while living in harmony with the natural flow of your life and abilities. Allow yourself to fulfill all the meaningful roles in your life, whatever that involves. So if you are a parent, a husband, a wife, a son or daughter, don't interfere: Be one with your life. Cherish the life that you have been given and open yourself to learning. As you flow with life, you participate in the Way; as you faithfully interact in living, you express Te.

> Those who trust
> The way of the world
> Are empowered by the world.
>> —*Tao Te Ching* 23, Grigg 1995, 91

Meditation on the Way

Sit quietly, eyes closed. Relax your thoughts and allow your uncon-scious mind to flow. Don't think about anything in particular as you relax very deeply. Feel your Oneness with everything around you, part of the flow of your life. Sense from within, without thought, in this moment, free and at peace. The winds of chi are stirring. The currents are within you. Use what you have well, and nothing will hold you back! Gather yourself in meditation and stay on your Path!

> If we follow the Tao
> Without doubt as we must
> Then all will thrive
> Through the power of trust
> In shadowy moments,
> Of uncertainty and fear,
> Place faith in the Way
> And the shadows will clear.
>> —C. Alexander Simpkins

Bibliography

Cain, Seymour. 1963. *Gabriel Marcel*. South Bend, Ind.: Regnery/ Gateway, Inc.

Chan, P. 1982. *How to Free Yourself from Pain*. Los Angeles: Price, Stern, Sloan.

Chan, W. T. 1963. *A Sourcebook in Chinese Philosophy*. Princeton, N.J.: Princeton University Press.

Chang Chung-yuan. 1963. *Creativity and Taoism*. New York: Harper Colophon Books.

Chang Po-tuan. 1987. *Understanding Reality: A Taoist Alchemical Classic*. Honolulu: University of Hawaii Press.

Chen, Ellen M. 1989. *The Tao Te Ching, A New Translation with Commentary*. St. Paul, Minn.: Paragon House.

Cheng, Man-ch'ing. 1981. *T'ai Chi Ch'uan*. Berkeley, Calif.: North Atlantic Books.

Cleary, T. 1991. *Vitality, Energy, Spirit: A Taoist Sourcebook*. Boston: Shambhala.

_____, trans. 2000. *Taoist Meditation: Methods for Cultivating a Healthy Mind and Body*. Boston: Shambhala.

Duke, M. 1972. *Acupuncture*. New York: Pyramid House.

Durant, Will. 1968. *The Story of Philosophy*. New York: Washington Square Press.

Duyvendak, J. J. L. 1992. *Tao Te Ching, The Book of the Way and Its Virtue*. Boston: Charles E. Tuttle Co., Inc.

Erickson, Milton, and Ernest Rossi. 1980. *The Collected Papers of Milton H. Erickson*. Vols. I-IV. New York: Irvington Publishers.

Evans, Richard I. 1981. *Dialogue with C. G. Jung*. New York: Praeger Publishers.

Farthing, G. William. 1992. *The Psychology of Consciousness*. New York: Prentice Hall.

Fogarty, J., trans. 1977. *A Barefoot Doctor's Manual: The AmericanTranslation of the Official Chinese Paramedical Manual*. Philadelphia: Running Press.

Freud, S. 1953-1974. *The Interpretation of Dreams*, Vol. IV in *The Standard Edition of the Complete Psychological Works of Sigmund Freud*. 24 Vols. London: Hogarth.

Fudler, S. 1989. *The Tao of Medicine*. Rochester, Vt.: Destiny Books.

Fung Yu-Lan. 1966. *A Short History of Chinese Philosophy*. New York: Free Press.

Gao, Duo, ed. 1997. *Chinese Medicine*. New York: Thunder's Mouth Press.

Gascoigne, Stephen. 1997. *The Chinese Way to Health: A Self-Help Guide to Traditional Chinese Medicine*. Boston: Tuttle Publishing.

Gerecht. Hope Karan. 1999. *Healing Design: Practical Feng Shui for Healthy and Gracious Living*. Boston: Tuttle Publishing.

Ghiselin, Brewster, ed. 1952. *The Creative Process*. New York: Mentor Books.

Giles, Lionel. 1959. *Taoist Teachings Translated from the Book of Lieh-Tzu*. London: John Murray.

Graham, A. C. 1990. *The Book of Lieh-tzu: A Classic of the Tao*. New York: Columbia University Press.

———. 1981. *Chuang-tzu: The Seven Inner Chapters and Other Writings from the Book Chuang-tzu*. London: George Allen & Unwin.

Grigg, Ray. 1995. *The New Lao Tzu: A Contemporary Tao Te Ching*. Boston: Charles E. Tuttle Co., Inc.

Groeger, J. A. 1984. "Evidence of unconscious semantic processing from a forced-error situation." *British Journal of Psychology* 75: 305–314.

Henricks, R. G. 1989. *Lao-tzu Te Tao Ching*. New York: Ballantine Books.

Herrigel, Eugen. 1971. *Zen in the Art of Archery*. New York: Vintage Books.

Hucker, C. O. 1975. *China's Imperial Past*. Stanford, Calif.: Stanford University Press.

Johnson, Jerry Alan. 1984. *The Masters Manual of Pa Kua Chang*. Pacific Grove, Calif.: Ching Lung Martial Arts Association.

Jung, C. G. 1978. *Psychology and the East*. Princeton, N.J.: Princeton University Press.

Kandinsky, Wassily. 1946. *On the Spiritual in Art*. New York: The Solomon R. Guggenheim Foundation.

Kaptchuk, T. J. 1983. *The Web That Has No Weaver: Understanding Chinese Medicine*. New York: Congdon & Weed.

Kaufmann, E., and B. Raeburn, eds. *Frank Lloyd Wright: Writings and Buildings*. New York: Meridan Books, 1960.

Kohr, Gary. 2001. *Living Chi: The Ancient Chinese Way to Bring Life Energy and Harmony into Your Life*. Boston: Tuttle Publishing.

Krenov, James. 1976. *A Cabinetmaker's Notebook*. New York: Van Nostrand Reinhold Company.

———. 1979. *The Impractical Cabinetmaker*. New York: Van Nostrand Reinhold Company.

Kubie, Lawrence. 1961. *Neurotic Distortion of the Creative Process*. New York: Farrar, Straus and Giroux.

Kuei, Steven, and Stephen Comee. 1997. *Beginning Gigong*. Boston: Tuttle Publishing.

Kwok, M. 1994. *Tao Te Ching*. New York: Barnes and Noble Books.

LaBerge, S. 1985. *Lucid Dreaming*. Los Angeles: Tarcher.

Lade, A. R., & J. Wong. 1987. *Chinese Massage: A Handbook of Therapeutic and Preventive Massage*. Point Roberts, Wash.: Hartley & Marks.

Lee, Ying-arng. 1968. *Lee's Modified Tai Chi for Health*. Hong Kong: Unicorn Press.

———. 1973. *Pa-Kua for Self-Defense*. Hong Kong: Unicorn Press.

Legge, J. 1962. *The Texts of Taoism*. 2 Vols. New York: Dover.

———. 1985. *The Chinese Classics*, Vol. 2. Oxford: Clarendon Press.

Liang, T. T. 1977. *T'ai Chi Ch'uan for Health and Self-Defense: Philosophy and Practice*. New York: Vintage Books.

Lin, Paul J. 1977. *A Translation of Lao Tzu's Tao Te Ching and Wang Pi's Commentary*. Ann Arbor: Center for Chinese Studies, University of Michigan.

Liu, Da. 1986. *T'ai Chi Ch'uan and Meditation*. New York: Schocken Books.

Luk, Charles. 1970. *Taoist Yoga: Alchemy and Immortality*. New York: Samuel Weiser Inc.

Mann, F. 1973. *Acupuncture: The Ancient Art of Healing and How It Works Scientifically*. New York: Vintage.

Meyer, Adolf. 1952. *The Collected Papers of Adolf Meyer*, Vol. IV. Baltimore, Md.: The Johns Hopkins Press.

Okakura, K. 1989. *The Book of Tea*. Tokyo: Kodansha International.

Palos, S. 1972. *The Chinese Art of Healing*. New York: Bantam.

People's Medical Publishing House of Beijing, China. 1984. *The Chinese Way to a Long and Healthy Life*. New York: Bell Publishing Company.

Robinet, Isabelle. 1993. *Taoist Meditation*. Albany: State University of New York Press.

Robinson, John Mansley. 1968. *An Introduction to Early Greek Philosophy*. Boston: Houghton Mifflin Company.

Rossbach, Sarah. 1987. *Interior Design with Feng Shui*. New York: E.P. Dutton.

Sailey, Jay. 1978. *The Master Who Embraces Simplicity: A Study of the Philosopher Ko Hung* A.D. 283-343. San Francisco: Chinese Materials Center, Inc.

Serizawa, K. 1989. *Tsubo: Vital Points for Oriental Therapy*. Tokyo: Japan Publications, Inc.

Shostrom, Everett, and Lawrence Brammer. 1968. *Therapeutic Psychology*. Englewood Cliffs, N.J.: Prentice Hall, Inc.

Siren, O. 1963. *The Chinese on the Art of Painting*. New York: Schocken Books.

Simpkins, C. Alexander, and Annellen M. Simpkins. 2000. *Simple Buddhism*. Boston: Tuttle Publishing.

———. 2000. *Simple Confucianism*. Boston: Tuttle Publishing.

———. 2000. *Effective Self-Hypnosis: Pathways to the Unconscious*. San Diego, Calif.: Radiant Dolphin Press.

———. 1999. *Simple Taoism*. Boston: Tuttle Publishing.

———. 1999. *Simple Zen*. Boston: Tuttle Publishing.

———. 1993. "Easy Does It: A Gentler, Kinder Approach to Stretching." *Inside Tae Kwon Do*. CFW Enterprises. August.

———. 1992. "May the Force Be with You." *Inside Karate Magazine*. Burbank, Calif.: C.F.W. Enterprises. August.

Siu, R. G. H. 1974. *Chi: A New-Taoist Approach to Life*. Cambridge, Mass.: The Massachusetts Institute of Technology.

Smith, Robert W. 1977. *Pa-Kua: Chinese Boxing for Fitness and Self-Defense*. Tokyo: Kodansha International Ltd.

———. 1974. *Hsing-I*. Tokyo: Kodansha International Ltd.

Ssu-ma, Ch'ien, and W. H. Nienhauser, ed. 1994. *The Grand Scribe's Records*. Vol. I. Bloomington: Indiana University Press.

_____. 1994. *The Grand Scribe's Records*. Vol. VII. Bloomington: Indiana University Press.

Suzuki, D. T. and Paul Carus. 1974. *The Canon of Reason and Virtue: Lao Tzu's Tao Teh King*. La Salle, Ill.: Open Court.

Sze, M. 1959. *The Way of Chinese Painting*. New York: Vintage Books.

Van Briessen, Fritz. 1998. *The Way of the Brush: Painting Techniques of China and Japan*. Boston: Tuttle Publishing.

Veninga, Louise. 1973. *The Ginseng Book*. Santa Cruz, Calif.: Ruka Publication.

Waley, A. 1958. *The Way and Its Power*. New York: Grove Weidenfeld.

Watanabe, J., and L. Avakian. 1984. *Secrets of Judo*. Boston: Charles E. Tuttle Co., Inc.

Watson, Burton. 1968. *The Complete Works of Chuang Tzu*. New York: Columbia University Press.

Watts, A. 1975. *Tao: The Watercourse Way*. New York: Pantheon Books.

Welch, H. 1957. *Taoism, The Parting of the Way*. Boston: Beacon Press.

Westwood, A., and O. Ratti. 1980. *Aikido and the Dynamic Sphere*. Boston: Charles E. Tuttle Co., Inc.

Wildish, Paul. 2000. *The Book of Ch'i*. Boston: Tuttle Publishing.

Wilhelm, H., and R. Wilhelm. 1995.*Understanding the I Ching*. Princeton, N.J.: Princeton University Press.

Wilhelm, R. 1990. *Tao Te Ching, The Book of Meaning and Life*. London: Arkana.

Wong, E. 1997a. *Harmonizing Yin and Yang: The Dragon-Tiger Classic*. Boston: Shambala.

———. 1997b. *The Shambhala Guide to Taoism*. Boston: Shambhala.

Wright, F. L. 1970. *The Natural House*. New York: Meridan Books.

Yang Jwing-ming. 1986. *Advanced Yang Style Tai Chi Chuan*. Vol. I & II. Jamaica Plain, Mass.: Yang's Martial Arts Academy (YMAA).

———. 1982. *Yang Style Tai Chi Chuan*. Los Angeles: Unique Publications.

———. 1990. *Chi Kung: Health and Martial Arts*. Jamaica Plain, Mass.: Yang Martial Arts Association (YMAA).

Yutang, L., ed. 1942. *The Wisdom of China and India*. New York: Random House.

———. 1948. *The Wisdom of Laotse*. New York: The Modern Library.

Ziyin, Shen, and Chen Zelin. 1994. *The Basis of Traditional Chinese Medicine*. Hong Kong: The Commercial Press.